ENFORCER

Also by Caesar Campbell

Wrecking Crew

ENFORCER

THE REAL STORY OF ONE OF AUSTRALIA'S MOST FEARED OUTLAW BIKERS

CAESAR CAMPBELL

with Donna Campbell

MACMILLAN

Pan Macmillan Australia

First published 2010 in Macmillan by Pan Macmillan Australia Pty Limited
1 Market Street, Sydney
Reprinted 2010, 2011, 2012 (three times), 2013

National Library of Australia
Cataloguing-in-Publication data:

Campbell, Caesar.

Enforcer / Caesar Campbell with Donna Campbell.
ISBN: 9781405040082 (pbk.)

Campbell, Caesar.
Bandidos (Gang).
Comancheros (Gang).
Motorcycle gangs – Australia.
Organized crime – Australia.
Criminals – Australia – Biography.

Other Authors/Contributors:
Campbell, Donna.

364.10660994

Typeset in 12.5/16pt Sabon by Midland Typesetters, Australia
Printed by McPherson's Printing Group

I would like to dedicate this book to my husband's brothers and their mum, Phyllis Campbell.
And to my parents, Max and Margaret Murrell.

—Donna Campbell

A Note From Donna

Never in my wildest dreams did I think I would meet a man like Caesar Campbell and end up living a biker lifestyle with him for more than three decades. This is why, over the years, I got Ceese to start telling me his stories. I took notes. We would laugh, I would cry, as the memories flowed. I started to think it would be a great way for our kids, our grandkids, my parents and friends to learn about this lifestyle, which is so different from their own. And also to fill them in on the real story behind what they called the Milperra Massacre. Then I thought it would make a great Christmas present for Caesar. A friend loaned me an old computer that I battered it all into before printing it up as a manuscript, covering our lives up to 1986. I never in a million years thought it would come out as a book, but a journalist rang Caesar one day and he seemed pretty interested in it all and he asked if we had any other stuff lying around. And that's how the manuscript found its way to publisher Tom Gilliatt at Pan Macmillan and into your hands.

This is what really happened. Some of the names have been changed.

—Donna Campbell

PERFECT DAY

Thunder of the Harley between my legs,
out with my brothers,
a full tank of gas,
my colours proud above all else.
My ol' lady on the back, the open highway.
Riding with my brothers.
The real deal,
being a Bandido.

—Caesar Campbell

PROLOGUE

SYDNEY, 1978

I'd left my lemon squash at the bar of the Ashfield Tavern and gone to have a leak when I was interrupted by John Boy, a bloke I'd just met from the Comancheros.

'Mate, there's some blokes out there trying to lift your bike onto a ute,' he said.

Out the front I found three of them with the front wheel of my customised Harley WLA up on their tray. I reached them just as they got the back wheel on.

'Whaddya think you're fuckin' doin'?' I said. 'Put the fuckin' bike back down.'

I didn't want them getting any dints in it, so I waited just long enough for them to sit it on the kickstand before – *whack* – I king-hit the bloke closest to me. He went down and I started stomping on his head. One of his

1

mates came at me and the adrenaline began to pump. I could feel the rush that came when I was outnumbered and the odds blew out. I grabbed the second bloke by the hair and bashed his head into the back of the ute. *Bang. Bang.* Still stomping on the bloke on the ground.

The third bloke was just about to jump on my back when John Boy stepped in and wrestled him to the ground, the two of them punching the shit out of each other. I finished off my two and picked up John Boy's bloke. Put a sleeper on him and he was out cold. I dropped him to the ground with his mates and John Boy went *boot*, right in the mouth. Teeth everywhere.

I pulled my boning knife from the sheath at the back of my belt. Curved, four-inch blade, perfect for boning rabbits. I took the first bloke's right hand and cut straight down at the base of his knuckle, slicing off his little finger. Then I did the same with his mates. Two of them were unconscious, but one wasn't. He voiced his objection fairly loudly.

I wrapped the fingers in my hanky and shoved them in my vest pocket. John Boy just looked at me.

'When cunts upset me I collect the odd finger or two,' I explained.

John Boy got on his bike and I got on mine. It had been good of him to help me out. He was from a different club, he didn't have to get involved.

'If there's ever anything I can do for ya,' I said to him, 'you got me word I'll do it.'

'Righto,' he nodded. 'I'll see ya round.'

I headed home. Walked in the door and threw the hanky at my old lady, Donna.

'Not more fingers,' she said. They went in the jar with the other twenty-odd.

At the time it seemed an unexceptional night. But seven years later, mourning the loss of two of my brothers, wanted for murder and banged up with a body full of bullets, I would look back on that night as where it all began. Now it's so obvious I can almost hear the gears crunching. My promise to John Boy, keeping my word; the revs as I switched clubs, and then the split. The acceleration as the crazy leader with a Napoleon complex and a wandering cock took us on his full-bore hell ride, wind in my hair, sun on my back, until we were rumbling into a pub car park in Milperra towards a shoot-out that would kill seven people. The Milperra Massacre, the newspapers called it.

I never call it that. I call it the ambush.

I always keep my word, but making that promise to John Boy was the biggest mistake I ever made.

CHAPTER 1

My grandfather, Joseph 'Joey' Campbell, was the light heavyweight boxing champion of the New South Wales police force. He once fought Les Darcy in an exhibition match in Newcastle to raise money to buy horses for the police, but apparently it turned into more than an exhibition match because both Darcy and my grandfather fancied the same woman, Margaret O'Brien. The ten-round bout was declared a draw, but my grandfather considered that he won the biggest prize, because he ended up with Margaret, my grandmother.

Joey was stationed at Barringun, north of Bourke on the New South Wales–Queensland border, and my grandmother used to tell me stories of waking up of a morning to camels in the vegetable patch. My grandfather would be gone for weeks at a time visiting the outlying properties and small settlements, accompanied by his old greyhound, Jack.

Joey only left the force because he got a boil on the back of his neck from the starched collars they used to wear in those days. The boil ended up going through his system and became a big carbuncle in his groin. They had to fly him from Barringun to Bourke hospital, but when they arrived they were told there'd been a fire and there was no anaesthetic available. The doctors reckoned that Joey had gone septic and if they didn't cut this carbuncle out he'd die. Granny said they brought in all the available men to hold him down and Joey, pumped full of sleeping tablets but no pain relief, just held on to the side of the bed while they cut this thing out. Unfortunately they cut a tendon too, so he ended up with his right leg shorter than his left. He was only three months short of retirement, but because he couldn't do those three months, the coppers never gave him the pension.

Joey was tough but my dad, George Campbell, was the toughest bloke I've ever known. He was six foot two inches and sixteen stone, and always into blues. He began his working life as a steelworker, and went on to have a trucking business; at one stage he owned three semitrailers. The funny thing, though, was that he was also a semi-pro tennis player in the Newcastle league. So Friday nights he'd be down the pub punching on, then come Saturday afternoon he'd be out running round in his little white shorts. That used to crack me up.

He spent a lot of time at the pub but he didn't really drink. He'd go there to meet his mates and play pool. His only indulgence was one shot glass of Johnnie Walker and a big cigar at night. That was it.

Dad was right into the Scottish ancestry of our family.

He traced our lineage to the Campbells of Cawdor and the Campbells of Argyll. He collected books and clippings about it all. He had this one book about the night the Campbells attacked the McDonalds. The Campbells apparently waited until the McDonalds had this shindig and were all drunk, then went and slit all the dogs' throats to silence their barking. The Campbells slipped into the castle and wiped out every McDonald there. The ensuing feud lasted for centuries. The first Campbell to be made a knight was called Colin Campbell, and that's why, when I was born, Dad named me Colin.

I was born in Newcastle, New South Wales, at the Mater Hospital on 18 July 1946. I don't know if I still hold the record but when I was born I was twenty-seven inches long and weighed nine pounds thirteen ounces. Mum said that was a big baby.

My mum, Phyllis, was a housewife, and one of the quietest, gentlest women you could meet. But she was probably one of the toughest women you'd ever want to meet too. She had to put up with my dad, and she had to put up with fourteen kids. There was me, then Wheels, and then another boy, Steven, but he only lived for two days. Mum said he was what they called a blue baby; his lungs didn't work. Then she had Bull, and the girls, then Shadow, Snake, Wack and Christopher.

My old man was gone a fair bit, on the road, but we were all pretty good for Mum because we knew what would happen when Dad got home if we'd been playing up. He used to have the razor strop – the leather strap you'd sharpen the old cutthroat razors on – and if you did something wrong it was into the bathroom, bend over the bath, and *whack, whack, whack* across the arse. He was real hard on me in the beginning. If he was in a bad mood, or something was broken or disappeared and no one owned up to it, being the eldest, I'd cop it. I'd know who did it and I'd be sitting there waiting for them to own up, but three-quarters of the time they never did. So I'd wait and even up with them later. If it was one of the girls I might let it go, but if it was one of my brothers I usually gave them a clip under the ear.

Mum was the opposite to the old man. She never raised a hand to one of us. She was only five foot two but she had this strong will about her. If my dad really went off the deep end and was going to clobber me she'd step in front and say, 'No, you're not going to touch him.' And my old man would turn round and walk off, swearing under his breath.

From the time I was about three years old my grandfather taught me to box. I even had the honour as a young fella of sparring with the legendary Dave Sands, who was a mate of my dad's and used to train at Henneberry's gym in Newcastle. He was middleweight champion of Australia and, along with Les Darcy, probably the best boxer ever to come out of this country, yet when I'd go in there with my dad he'd spend an hour with me giving me tips on how to box. He used to float around like Sugar Ray Robinson. He had this natural ability where everything seemed to come easy to him. Fred Henneberry – himself a former Australian middleweight champion – and Dave were always trying to talk my old man into becoming a pro fighter. He never did, but he knew all these blokes that were around the boxing – Dave and Kid Griffo, and the famous wrestler

Strangler Lewis – and I was lucky enough to learn a lot off them.

The first time I backed up my old man in a fight I was twelve years old. A car ran us off the road, four blokes got out, and Dad was into them. One of them had him in a choke hold and I was thinking, Oh shit, what can I do? There was a big screwdriver on the floor of the car so I grabbed it and stabbed this bloke in the arse. Put it in about an inch. He let go of my old man and was chasing me around the car, trying to pull this screwdriver out. From then on the old man would take me with him if he was going to get into a fight and he might be outnumbered. He had these two vicious bull terriers and it was my job to hold the dogs. Dad would go into the pub and offer a bloke out the front. The bloke would come out with his mates and I'd be standing there with these dogs foaming at the mouth. My old man would say to the bloke, 'Righto, it's me and you or I turn the dogs loose.' If Dad was winning, I held them. If someone started to get over the top of him I turned them loose. That evened up the fight.

He never went into a pub wanting to get into a fight but he had a real fiery temper. If someone said some- thing about him or gave him a dirty look – it only had to be the smallest thing – that was it. He was a real proud bloke and if he thought he'd been insulted, he wanted to even up. But he got into most of his fights because he'd always stick up for his mates. He used to say to me, 'Don't do what I do. You'll always be in blues. I know half me mates are cockheads, but if I'm with them, I've got to help 'em out.' Blokes used to take advantage of that. They knew my old man would back them up.

Along with the boxing, I was the captain of the rugby league team all through primary school, and I owned a couple of horses. I spent a fair bit of time hanging around Tracey's riding school up at Merewether. A lot of sheilas hung around Tracey's with their own horses and that's where I met a chick called Diane. She was nineteen and I was thirteen, but at thirteen I was five foot eleven. We were out at a place called the Blue Lagoon and she put it on me. I thought all my Christmases had come at once. It was all over in about sixty seconds, but from then on I found that having a horse helped you get the sheilas. It was the same with bikes.

My first encounter with a Harley was when my mate Trevor and I found an old WLA in the back of his dad's plumbing warehouse. The WLA was a military model Harley-Davidson produced around World War II. We tinkered with it until we got it going, then we'd ride around in paddocks and stormwater channels at the back of Trevor's place. We kept it hidden in Trevor's shed. If Dad had found out about it he'd have killed me. His best mate had been killed on a WLA so he hated bikes.

There was a motorcycle club in Newcastle called the Spot Boys and we used to see fifteen of these blokes coming down the main street of Hamilton, an inner-city suburb, on their Triumphs and Beezers. It was just a mad feeling seeing them riding together. I liked the way people all looked at them whenever they rode by. They had the leather jackets with their patch painted on the back, the flying scarves and leather chaps. Slicked-back rock'n'roll hair. Just like Marlon Brando in *The Wild One*. I thought, Oh shit, don't that look good.

They used to go to the pub across from the fun parlour where we'd hang out, and I got to know one of the blokes, Four Fingers Jack. I was telling him about the old WLA and he said, 'So where is it?' I told him it was at Trevor's, and he put me on the back of his Triumph to ride over there. Well that was it. Once I was on the back of his Triumph I knew: this was what I wanted to be.

At the time, though, I was still at the Marist Brothers' high school in Hamilton, vice-captain of the football team, focused on my horses and the boxing. I took one of my mares, an ex-riding school horse called Apache, to the Royal Newcastle Show. She was that quiet you could slide down her back, crawl under her legs and lie beneath her. She was a top horse and won first prize in the quietest horse category. Later at the show, we came across a boxing tent with a little thick-set bloke in a bowler hat, spruiking out the front, banging a drum. My old man wanted me to have a go, but I was only fourteen so I wasn't keen. Dad wasn't going to take no for an answer, though, and there was a young fighter in the troupe who only looked about twenty, so I decided I might have a chance against him.

You had to go three rounds, but in the second round I clocked this bloke, he went down on his bum and didn't want to get back up. I won a quid.

I went through to about third form at the Marist Brothers'. I was in woodwork class one day and everyone hated doing woodwork because the teacher was so creepy and strict. This day I put my plane down the wrong way and he decided to give me six with the cane.

11

I put my hands out to get six and he said, 'No, turn them over the other way.' So I copped six across the knuckles. I must have said something under my breath as I was walking away, because he said, 'Campbell, back here.'

'What for?'

'You're getting another six,' he said.

'Like fuck I am. You can go and get rooted.' And I walked out.

Mum got the phone call so by the time I'd walked home the old man knew. Soon as I walked in the door I could see I was going to cop it.

'Hold on! Hold on!' I said. 'It wasn't my fault.'

'You got ten seconds to tell me why not,' he said.

I told him the story.

'Really?'

He went down to the school, fronted the woodwork teacher and flattened him.

That was the end of school for me. After that I helped Mum around the house and went along on jobs with the old man. He continued training me with the boxing and introduced me to knife fighting. Taught me how to hold a knife properly, how to block, how to slash with a blade rather than stab. He always drummed into me, 'You never want to kill someone in a knife fight. If you can get out of it, do, otherwise you'll end up locked up for life.' So he showed me the best spots to target to disable a person (across the bicep and, if you could get down to it, the Achilles tendon), and the places to avoid so as not to kill them (the jugular and the femoral artery in the leg). I don't know where Dad learnt all that stuff. Just growing up I suppose. He also showed me how the corner of the old matchboxes were so sharp that if you slashed down hard at the right angle it was like using a razor. The coppers couldn't figure out for a long time how all these people with such bad wounds were getting them.

Not long after I quit school, we left the Newcastle area and moved around a bit. We went to Toukley, Ettalong and Umina on the New South Wales central coast, then to North Narrabeen, Narrabeen and Dee Why on Sydney's northern beaches. I was fifteen when I got work on a fishing boat, then as an offsider to a milko, but the jobs never lasted long because we were always moving. I don't know why we shifted around so much. Dad never told us. But we never stayed anywhere more than a few months. Next thing we kids knew we'd be packing up all the bunk beds and moving again.

We ended up down in Victoria, at a big guesthouse on ten acres called Sassafras Lodge. It had six bungalows out the back, and ten or twelve bedrooms in the main house. Seeing as my old man wasn't using it as a guesthouse, I took one of the guest rooms down the far end of the house.

Even though I was seventeen by this stage, my old man used to insist I be home by eleven pm. That was his rule. So I'd dutifully return by eleven, but then I'd go down to my room, where I had this German shepherd called Zig. He was the biggest shepherd you've ever seen and he was trained so that if anyone came near me he'd rip them to pieces. I would put Zig on watch, and the old man knew he couldn't come into the room or the dog would get him. Hence he didn't check on me. I'd go out the window and back down to my mate's. We'd drive around in someone's car or get the bikes and go for a ride.

One night we were driving through Box Hill in my mate Johnny Nankervis's FJ when we were attacked by about eight cars. Johnny did a U-ey and headed for home, but four cars kept up the chase and ran us off the road. As soon as the FJ went into the bank on the side of the road, Johnny and my other mates all hit the toe and I was left there to punch on by myself. I grabbed this great hunk of wood that was lying on the side of the road and laid into everyone that came near me.

After a while they chucked it in and pissed off in their cars. I had to hitch home, which meant I didn't get back until about two in the morning. I was sneaking in the back door when the old man piped up, 'Is that you?'

'Yeah, but I've got a good reason.'

I had my hand just inside the doorjamb, and he booted the door, crushing my hand. My hand was killing me but I went inside and told him what had happened.

'Oh, all right,' he said. 'Go to bed and I'll talk to you when you get up.'

Next day he bandaged my hand and asked, 'Would you know any of these blokes if you saw 'em?'

'I'd know two of the cars.'

So that night we went down to Box Hill – Dad with a pick handle – and I spotted the two cars parked outside a milk bar. Dad walked into the milk bar, smashed every bloke in the place, then came out and smashed their headlights and windscreens before hopping back in the car.

'When you grow up,' he said, 'that's how you do it.'

'Yeah, okay Dad.'

AFTER YEARS of boxing, in Victoria I moved into the wrestling scene. I found that the wrestling could outdo the boxing because, when you're a boxer, you really just learn to throw punches, but if you're a wrestler, you can grab a person, get him in close, and put arm locks on him, leg locks, head locks. You can immobilise a person in so many ways. And when you combine the boxing skills with the wrestling, it sets you up to be a very strong fighter.

At seventeen, I won the Victorian under-twenty-one Greco-Roman championship, but I came away with a more lasting legacy, too. I met an old Italian bloke who'd been a champion wrestler in Europe, and he said to me, 'The way you wrestle, you wrestle like gladiator. You like little Caesar.' After that people started calling me Little Caesar, and before long they dropped the 'little'. From then on I was known as Caesar.

I bought myself an AJS 500 twin bike, had my hair styled in an Elvis peak, and started hanging round a motorcycle club called Bad Blood from Emerald at the bottom of the Dandenong Ranges, near where we were living. They'd started back in 1941 as the first outlaw club in Australia. They weren't a big club, but that's how they liked it, small and real tight.

They were mad as cut snakes. They were always in blues and caused themselves a lot of trouble with the local coppers. They used to do things that I wouldn't do. They'd switch off their headlights at ten o'clock at night and scream down these roads through Sherbrooke Forest. I thought, Fuck this. If a truck came round a corner you were gone.

We used to go for runs together or meet up at milk bars and play pool, put songs on the jukebox. I was just about to become a nominee for them when my old man decided the family was moving back to New South Wales. I could have stayed in Victoria, but Dad was getting pretty crook with diabetes and a bad heart, so I'd been helping him out a lot and we'd become real close.

We ended up back on Sydney's northern beaches, at Avalon and then Dee Why, then shifted to Dulwich Hill and Surry Hills in the inner city. While we were living in Surry Hills, Mum went into the Women's Hospital to have her last babies, the twins, Cathy and Pauline. It was 1965 and I had just got my first tattoo. It was a panther on my arm, but Dad absolutely hated tattoos, so I had to keep my shirt sleeves rolled right down to hide it from him. I went to visit Mum in the hospital and for some unknown reason, sitting there opposite Dad, I started rolling up my sleeves.

Dad sharpened his focus. 'What the shit is that?'

Whoomp, I was off, hotfooting it out of the hospital with the old man after me. I was nineteen and Dad was crook, but I wasn't taking him on. He was still the toughest bloke I'd ever run into.

No matter how sick Dad got, he was still a mad bluer and wasn't going to take crap from anyone. If someone insulted him or put the family down, he didn't care how bad his heart was, he'd want to punch on or get even. He came home from a pub at Taylor Square one day in a pretty bad way, spewing and not real well. I got it out of him that this bloke and four of his mates had ganged up on him. I knew who the bloke was, and knew that he walked past the same factory in Surry Hills every afternoon. We went down there and I hid in the doorway while my old man waited out the front of the factory. This bloke eventually turned up with a mate of his and obviously thought they were going to do the old man over again. Well I grabbed them and dragged them inside the entrance alcove and gave them a good hiding. Then I said to the old man, 'All right, Dad, do what you wanna do.' The old man could hardly make it up the steps, but he got up and gave them a kicking.

Another time we were driving together when he spotted a bloke who'd pissed him off. The old man pulled over and I grabbed the bloke and had him in the back. The old man was saying, 'Punch him in the ear, belt him there, twist this, break that.' I ended up breaking both his thumbs, a couple of fingers on each hand, and thumping the shit out of him. Then we threw him out of the car at about thirty miles an hour. He bounced down the road.

MEANWHILE I was doing a bit of work driving utes and vans, doing deliveries. But my old man had a lot of friends up at Kings Cross and I started picking up some work from them. I think he got to know them through his trucking business; he did a lot of carting interstate. Some of them were on the shady side, but to Dad, that was their business. Dad never got charged with a crime, he never went to jail. He got on as well with some of the top cops as he did with the blokes at the Cross. It was funny, one night we'd have the regional police commander over for tea and the next it would be a well-known underworld identity. I think Dad was respected because he had the balls to say no to a lot of stuff that people wanted him to do. And he would never tell the coppers a thing about the people he knew up the Cross. He had his own code, which was loyalty and honour.

The Cross became my main haunt. It was buzzing from all the American Marines on R&R from Vietnam. There was rock'n'roll at Surf City, illegal casinos, the transvestite stage show Les Girls and the Whiskey Au Go Go Nightclub on William Street. There were characters like the strip-joint spruiker 'Half a Mo' who wore funny-coloured suits and a bowler hat; strippers like Alexander the Great who had the biggest tits in the Cross; and the most famous of them all, Sandra Nelson at the Pink Pussycat. I took out Bambi, the second most famous stripper in town. Chequers nightclub was for the posh types. No bikers allowed, but Dad and I were allowed in.

Behind it all were the standover men like Chow Hayes and Chicka Reeves. And then there were the big players above them.

I was coming out of the dark backrooms of the Carousel Club on business one time when I bumped into a very well-known underworld boss surrounded by bodyguards. He turned to me and said, 'You're Caesar.'

'Yeah. And I know who you are.'

'If you're ever looking for a bit of work, get in contact with me through the club here.'

He was known as the Little King, and from then on I worked for him – collecting and doing other bits and pieces. The going rate for most collectors was ten per cent, but I used to charge thirty-five per cent, so I'd get the real hard jobs, retrieving money from people who'd purchased goods and hadn't paid for them. Not straights, these were people on the other side of the law. I wouldn't go near a straight.

WE UPPED and moved again, this time to Annandale in Sydney's inner west. It was pretty rough around there in 1966. There was a local bowling alley that was known as Blood Alley because if you were there on a Friday or Saturday night you'd have three or four groups of blokes punching on. They didn't give a stuff that there were families there with kids.

We had one gang up the street that considered themselves to be real heavies. Sometimes there'd be twenty or thirty of them hanging round of a weekend. I was at home one day when someone came in and said one of these blokes had pulled a gun on my younger brother. I was straight out the door, running as fast as I could, but who was already halfway up the street in front of me? My mum. She got there just before me and grabbed the barrel of the gun. The bloke was standing there in shock, so I pushed Mum out of the way and grabbed the gun off him. I hit him straight in the face with it and just kept pounding till he went down. Another couple of them came out and I did the same with them. Then I unloaded the gun and threw it over their roof.

From then on whenever they saw one of us it was a running blue. By this stage the old man was so crook he'd taken to carrying a big shifter and a bottle of ammonia in his back pocket, so that if he got into a blue he could throw the ammonia in the bloke's face to blind him and take his breath away, then lay into him with the shifter. This one time he was on the main drag, Parramatta Road, when he ran into some of them and pulled out his tools.

He put a few of them away and came home but they must have got on the blower because next thing about thirty of them turned up and were mobbing up the end of the street. The old man told Mum to boil up some water on the stove, so she was filling up the pots, and all these blokes were marching down the street and banging on the front wall. We had an eight–foot cyclone fence topped with barbed wire, which some of these blokes were trying to scale. The old man and I were belting them with pick handles.

Dad yelled out to Mum to tip the water, so she and my sister Patricia started pouring the boiling water from the second-storey windows. These blokes were jumping up and down while Dad and I kept laying into them. One bloke got halfway over and my German shepherd leapt up and grabbed him by the leg. He was stuck on the barbed wire, with my shepherd hanging off his leg. It only ended when the coppers turned up after about fifteen minutes.

* * *

STRAIGHT ACROSS the road from us at Annandale lived a couple of sisters, Sandra and Cathy. Sandra was seventeen and one of those real glamour-type sheilas who would have the blokes hanging off her left, right and centre. Even my sister's boyfriend wanted to go out with her. I was up the milk bar one day buying a couple of bottles of Coke when she walked in and said, 'Caesar, how come you've never asked me out?'

'Because I don't fuckin' like ya.' I turned around and walked out of the shop.

I'd seen the way she treated her younger sister Cathy like shit so I didn't want a bar of her. Cathy was fifteen and a pretty good-looking girl, and she had a really nice personality. I used to spend an hour or two each day sitting on the step with Cathy outside her joint because I felt sorry for her. A week before her sixteenth birthday she came up to me and said, 'Do you wanna do something for me for me birthday?'

'What?'

'Will you go to bed with me?'

'Yeah all right.'

She was a nice sheila and we started hanging out together. She fell pregnant and started to show. One day my old man finally asked me, 'Are you the father of Cathy's kid?'

'Yeah.'

'Well you're gunna have to marry her.'

The old man marched me down to the house and Cathy came out. The old man said, 'Do you wanna marry him?'

'Yes, I'd love to,' she said.

Then her mother came out: 'Your bikie scum's not getting anywhere near my daughter.'

The old man cast his eye over Cathy. 'Well it looks like he already has.'

That was the end of it for Cathy and me. Her parents forbade her from seeing me, which was a shame because I liked her a lot, so after a while I hooked up with this other bird, Irene. It was more out of convenience than anything. Irene's girlfriend was going out with a mate of mine, Pete Davies, so we were all knocking around together. Pete was into bikes and we used to go riding a lot. His old man owned a car yard and if ever I needed a flashy car like a Corvette or a Jag or a Porsche I only had to ring him up and say, 'I see you got a new Ferrari in there.'

'When do you want it?'

I'd rock out there and leave my bike in his garage, pick up the Ferrari and go for a pose up the Cross.

Irene had just come onto the scene when I took her home one day. My old man gave us the big speech: 'Just remember, you get her pregnant, you gotta marry her.'

'Yeah, Dad.'

Next thing I knew she was pregnant. She told my old man before she even told me.

I was spewing. There was just nothing between us. As far as I was concerned she'd cracked on to me. But the old man was on at me: 'You gotta do the right thing.' I thought, Here it comes.

Even though, as a kid, my old man had belted me from pillar to post, I had that much respect for him that there was just no way the thought ever entered my head to fight back. If someone else had belted me I'd have ripped their head off, but if Dad'd belted me in the mouth, I'd have stood there and taken it.

So at twenty-one I married Irene. Meanwhile Cathy had given birth to a baby boy, Michael Anthony, and had taken to wheeling the pram past the house to piss off Irene. It worked.

I would have liked to have spent time with Cathy and the baby, but Cathy's parents eventually moved her away from me and we lost contact.

On 11 March 1969, Irene gave birth to a baby boy, too. We named him Chane, and as much as there was nothing between me and Irene I was very proud to have a son.

Within a few months of Chane's arrival my old man's heart finally gave up and he died at the age of forty-six. We were really close at the end, and for the first time in my life I shed a tear.

I was twenty-two and took over the role of looking after the family. Mum still had thirteen kids at home, including me, right down to Cathy and Pauline, who were only three years old.

The older brothers were all bringing in a bit of money: I was still collecting for the Little King, Wheels was driving trucks, Bull and Shadow were putting up sheds, doing some brickie's labouring. Everyone was chipping in. I didn't have to do much in the way of discipline. Once my brothers got to seventeen or eighteen they were out doing their own thing and getting into blues. I just did my best to make sure they didn't end up in hospital or jail.

CHAPTER 2

Since returning to Sydney I'd been keeping my eye on the outlaw motorcycle scene, hoping to find a club I liked. A lot of bikers from different clubs hung round the Cross – it was neutral territory – and I got to know a fair few of them. There were no real big clubs at the time, just a lot of smaller ones like the Executioners and Corporation of Sin. None of them took my fancy so Irene's brother, Lurch, said to me, 'Why don't we start our own club?'

'Yeah, why don't we?'

We sat down and thought about a name and came up with Gladiators. 'That'd be a good name,' Lurch said, 'because you're Caesar, and Caesar used to be in charge of the gladiators.'

We checked round the area to see if the name was taken. It wasn't, so I designed a patch – 'the colours' – with a gladiator sticking his sword into a tiger raised up on its hind legs. We made it blue with maroon lettering, then had it drawn up and embroidered, and sewn onto our leather vests (the deck, or cut-off). I also had the colours tattooed onto my back. By then I was growing my hair real long and had the beard.

The Gladiators officially started up in July 1969, with me as president and Lurch as vice-president. Lurch was a pretty wild-looking bloke, even bigger than me and with nearly 500 tattoos. Even his ears and face were tattooed.

Our territory took in the inner-western suburbs of Ashfield and Five Dock, plus we shared Burwood with Corporation of Sin, because I'd become mates with their president, Les Markham, up at the Venus Room in the Cross and he was a top bloke. Our pub was the Illinois at Five Dock.

The Gladiators didn't bother with initiation ceremonies or anything like that. I've always been of the opinion that you don't need a whole lot of rules to run a club. The main rules were honour, courage and you didn't do the wrong thing by your brother. Being in a motorbike club in those days wasn't about money and who had the bigger house. It was about the fun of riding together and the honour of the brotherhood. So we stuck to those three rules, and everyone understood what they meant. You knew by honour that you didn't go round picking on straights. Honour meant you didn't give up your brother. If a bloke wore the same colours as you, you honoured him, and that included honouring his old lady. I found in some clubs that members used to put shit on other members' old ladies. That's not good for club morale and it's putting down your brother.

You knew by courage that you never let your brother

down, you always backed him up no matter what. There could be forty blokes wanting to punch on and just you and two of your brothers, but you stayed there till the end. You might end up in hospital with your head kicked in but you never left your brother.

And you knew that doing the right thing by your brother meant that you didn't rip him off in a deal over a bike and you never tried to crack on to his old lady.

An outlaw club in those days was really strict, and its members more honourable than the normal straight; if a member did something really wrong he'd be kicked out of the club. Contrary to popular opinion, clubs just didn't tolerate members going round raping sheilas or bashing blokes who were walking down the street with their missus and kids. You'd have to have a good reason to front the club if you got into a blue with anyone, and rules were strictly enforced.

THE CAMPBELL family continued to grow later that year when my brother Shadow's good mate came to live with us. Chop was sixteen and had been kicked out of home eighteen months earlier. He'd been living on the streets, sleeping in parks and bus shelters. We were living at Lethbridge Park in Sydney's outer west by then, and when Mum heard Chop's story she asked him to move in. It didn't worry her having another mouth to feed; he just got thrown into one of the bunks and became another brother. It was like he was making up for the son Mum had lost after birth.

From the get-go we all considered Chop one of us, but he had his doubts, so we went through the blood-brother ceremony like in the westerns. Everyone cut their hand, and I mean a decent cut. I still have the scar today. Chop cut his, and we mixed the blood. Then we all dripped some blood into a cup and Chop drank it. Well after that he had Campbell blood running through him and that made him as much a Campbell as the rest of us. He considered himself a true family member. He started calling himself Mark Campbell, and when he turned eighteen he officially changed his name. Whenever anyone mentioned his life before he joined the Campbells he would go right off the deep end. I saw him flatten people over it. And you didn't want to make Chop mad because although he was short, he was thick-set with muscles on his muscles, and when he got into a fight, he liked to bite his opponent's ear off. Even if he knocked a bloke out cold, he wasn't happy till he'd taken that ear. He'd bend down, chomp it off and spit it into the gutter. Hence the name Chop.

My own little family was growing too, with the birth of another son, Lee, followed later by two daughters, Peggy and Samantha. I loved spending time with the kids, but Irene was another story, so most of my days were taken up working and with the Gladiators.

As EACH of my brothers got his licence, he came into the Gladiators. First up was Wheels, who was the strongest of the brothers, six foot six and 140 kilos. One time he held up a V8 ute while I changed the tyre. Then came Bull, big and strong with a chest as broad as a bull's. He was a hard one to set off, but if you did set him off you were in trouble. Next up was Shadow. He was real quiet, a lot like me. As a kid he was always following me around, which is why the old man called him Shadow. Dad used to say me and Shadow were the nicest of the lot but, once provoked, we became the nastiest.

Chop joined up of course, and then Snake, who was a real bad-tempered bastard. You got on the wrong side of Snake and you were in for a great deal of pain. And then there was Wack, the youngest to join (although we also had an even younger brother, Christopher). He was another quiet one, but we called him Wack because he could drop you with either hand.

We were over at the Ashfield Tavern one night when Chop got into a blue with one of the bouncers. The Ashfield Tavern was a bit of a slaughterhouse at the time and Chop got glassed in the back. Luckily it was only in the shoulder, but he was spewing. It would've been on, but the cops turned up so we hit the toe.

We went back two nights later looking for the bouncer – me, Chop, Bull and Wack. This bouncer was just coming in to work, and Chop went straight up to him, *bang*. Knocked him down to the ground, jumped on top of him, and started smashing into him. Bull and I thought Chop was going to kill this bloke so we tried to pull him off. I had one arm and a leg, Bull had the other arm and leg. We were pulling him up, but of course Chop had sunk his teeth right into the bloke's ear and jaw. Latched on like a bull terrier and wasn't letting go. So as we were trying to pull him off, the bloke was actually coming up off the ground in Chop's mouth. We tried to shake Chop loose but all we ended up doing was shaking him that much that the bloke's ear came off in Chop's mouth. Bloody Chop got up, spat it out, gave the bouncer another kick in the ribs, and we were away.

I NEVER went out of my way to look for fights. My old man always taught me that the blokes who can really fight don't go looking for fights; they don't have to prove how good they are because they know how good they are. But there are some fights you can't walk away from: if someone really puts it on you, they insult your wife or your family or your club, you need to defend your honour. And when you've got the hair and the tatts and the leathers, fights seem to come looking for you. All these blokes want to take on the big bad bikie. There were times when I'd cross the road because I saw blokes coming and I knew there was going to be a blue. They could be seventeen- or eighteen-year-old kids, pissed, and I could never see the point in beating up someone you knew you could beat.

One day at the Illinois, there was a little bloke about five foot nine, sixty kilos. He had his missus with him, but for some reason he was looking for trouble. I was in there and I was in training, built like a brick shithouse. Twenty-inch arms, fifty-seven-inch chest. He came over to me and he was drunk as a skunk. And he said, 'I could kick the shit outta you.'

'Yeah, all right, mate.'

He wandered off, but was back soon enough. 'I could kick the shit outta you.'

'Yeah, yeah, you probably could.'

When he came back the third time I thought, Ugh, so I walked into the next bar. Five minutes later he was in there. 'I could kick the shit outta you.'

I decided to leave.

I was walking through the toilets that connected the lounge to the front bar, when he grabbed my cut-off. As soon as he put his hands on my colours I thought, You've done the wrong thing now, pal.

I grabbed him by the hair and the belt, took him into one of the cubes, stuck his head in the toilet and flushed it. I could have kicked the shit out of him but it wouldn't have proven anything because I could have beaten him with one finger.

To me, a good fight is one where you're not sure if you're going to be the winner. That's when the adrenaline starts pumping. Sometimes you might take on three or four blokes. The bigger the odds, the bigger the rush. That's the fight I like getting into. If I know I'm going to win, what's the point? I'm just going to skin my knuckles.

And I like the fighting when it's an all-in brawl. Anything can happen in an all-in. Or a knife fight, I love knife fights. Most people think if you've got a blade it's just a matter of sticking someone, stabbing them. But it's not. There's a real art to using a knife and using it well, and I was lucky enough to have been taught that art. To feel your knife slicing someone or even feeling your own skin getting sliced – it's something that's hard to explain. I always felt like I was out of my body. I lapped up the pain. That's when I zoned out. Everything went red and then black, and then it was over. And the other bloke was all carved up.

I was up at Kings Cross one time and this bloke had been following me round all night. Up and down the main street of the Cross, just like the bloke in the Illinois, telling me how he could belt the crap out of me.

'Yeah, mate.' I didn't want to get into a blue in the main street of the Cross, but he was really starting to piss me off.

Finally I walked down Springfield Avenue and thought, All right, if you're gunna keep following me you can cop it where no one's gunna see.

I turned down the laneway alongside the Manzil Room, and once we were partway along I just turned and went *whack*. He staggered back. *Whack*. I hit him in the throat. He went down and was bouncing round on the ground like he was having a fit. I was watching him, and for some reason I thought, Fuck it. I pulled out the Aitor, a Spanish survival knife I used to carry on my right hip. I put my boot on his wrist, bent over the bloke's hand, pressed down hard on the blade, and severed his thumb.

That was the first digit I ever took, but I threw it away on the way home. I thought, What am I gunna do with it? But later I was telling Shadow the story and he said, 'If you're gunna do that you oughta get a jar of formaldehyde so you can keep 'em.' It sounded like a good idea so I picked up some formaldehyde from a funeral home and started carrying a boning knife in a sheath on the back of my belt. The Aitor wasn't really up to the job of severing fingers.

Before too long I was down at the old Rock'n'Roll pub at Woolloomooloo (better known these days as the Woolloomooloo Bay Hotel) and got into a punch-up with these two big Islanders. It turned out to be not a bad fight. One of them was stung on the ground, but then the other bloke got me from behind and stuck his finger in my eye, trying to gouge it out. I thought, Fuck you. I slipped my arm under his, got my hip under him and threw him onto the concrete. I had blood coming out of my eye and could hardly see. Righto, so out with the knife. Took his forefinger, then took his mate's little finger. They were both still conscious. Took the digits home and they were the first to go into the jar.

It became a little thing of mine that when someone pissed me off I'd take a finger. If they pissed me off a real lot, I'd take a thumb.

By 1971 the Gladiators were rolling along so we decided it was time to get ourselves a clubhouse. We found an old federation place in Queens Road, Five Dock, which was going pretty cheap because the previous tenants had wrecked the joint. There were some smashed windows and they'd knocked out a wall. It suited us because we would have knocked out the wall anyway to make the room bigger, and we had blokes in the club like Lurch, who was a bricklayer and carpenter, and Bull and Shadow, who'd done construction work. Between them they could virtually rebuild a house, so the mess didn't bother us. Lurch and the blokes did it up. We kept two of the bedrooms for anyone who needed a place to stay, and converted the other two bedrooms into a bar and the shag room. Any bloke who turned up with his stray could use that room.

We kept the club pretty small. It was hard to find blokes that my brothers wanted in the club because they used to judge everyone solely on their fighting ability.

I was more of the opinion that a bloke should be judged on how good he would be for the club, and what he could bring to the club. But Wheels, Bull, Shadow, Snake and Wack thought that if a bloke couldn't fight, he should hit the highway. The problem was that to find blokes who could fight as good as my brothers was practically impossible. To this day, I think there's probably been two that have been beaten once. One of them was dead drunk, and the other one had about five on him and got hit in the head with a steel rubbish bin.

Nevertheless, hanging round the Cross we managed to pick up a few nominees. One was a bloke by the name of Schultz who was a minder for the girls they had working above the Venus Room. If anyone started roughing up one of the girls he'd throw them down the stairs. He could fight, and he was a big boy. He was a power lifter. We'd see him at the gym bench pressing 600 pounds. I was round at his flat one day, and he had this industrial blender. He chucked in nearly half a tin of protein powder and some milk, and drank what must have been two or three litres of protein drink, then scoffed two chooks and a slab of tuna.

He bought himself a Rigid Sporty, which is like a chopper, and got himself acquainted with his new wheels. Each time the bike went down he'd grab it round the frame with one hand and just pick it up off the ground. We'd all be standing there in awe, just looking at him. He was a monster, with a chest like a barrel and no neck. When we went shopping to get him a vest to put his colours on, the biggest one they had wouldn't go halfway round Schultz. They had to get a whole skin in to customise a vest for him.

I remember one night up at the Venus Room we got word that all the bouncers in the Cross were coming to get the Gladiators. The story went that a renowned underworld figure had hired them because Chop had beaten up his son over some sheila.

We sat there waiting for these bouncers. The Venus Room had a real narrow hallway that you had to walk down to get into the main bar, so we figured that if these bouncers came for us, we'd just stand at the end of the hallway and bash them two at a time as they reached us.

Well, we saw all these Maoris coming down, and at the time most of the bouncers up the Cross were Maoris. So we started bashing them. Bull had a chain, Shadow had a baseball bat, and we were pounding the shit out of them, bodies everywhere. Then all of a sudden Wack yelled out, 'Hang on! Hang on! Have a look at their legs.' Nearly every one of them was wearing shorts and socks. Turned out it was actually two grades of a rugby union team. They'd come over from New Zealand to play some district clubs out here, walked into the Venus Room for a night out, and had the shit pounded out of them.

We helped them up and called the ambulance then took off before the cops showed up.

ONE NIGHT in 1972 I was riding back through Haymarket in town when I came across a bunch of wogs belting this young boy of about ten and trying to drag his older sister into their car. I hopped off the bike and gave the four blokes a hiding.

The young sheila was terrified so I asked her where she lived.

'About two blocks from here.'

'I'll ride me bike real slow and walk ya home.'

I had my feet on the ground, the bike more or less idling along. When we got there she said, 'You come upstairs, meet my grandfather.'

I took my bike up in the freight elevator and rolled it out into this big room set up with heavy bags and large cane baskets. It turned out to be a kyite studio and her grandfather was the sensei. Kyite is a North Korean martial art not normally taught to Europeans, but the sensei was so grateful I'd helped his grandkids that he offered to teach me.

The art of kyite is to destroy your opponent. There's none of this self-defence, search-for-enlightenment business like in *The Karate Kid*. Your defence is that you go in and beat the shit out of the other bloke, so that he can't hurt you. The baskets in the studio were full of barley or wheat, and once you'd learnt the correct technique you could use your fist or, more commonly in kyite, your palm, to drive your arm through the grain right up to your elbow. Which meant you could hit pretty hard.

Kyite also finessed my knife skills, teaching the art of fighting in really close with a small curved blade, like a skinning knife, that can cut and rip at the same time. You're trained to block out everything around you and just concentrate on the knife in front of you so that after a while it becomes automatic and you don't have to think about it, you just do it.

I got up to a fifth-degree black belt, having added

some nice new skills to my fighting repertoire. And I was about to get the chance to put some of those skills to use.

I'D HEARD up the Cross about an underground fighting scene run by my boss, the Little King. So I got in contact with him and asked if he could get me into it. I had to give him my word I'd never mention anything about him or the fighting to anyone, not even my brothers. Then it was just a matter of waiting for a phone call.

It might have been a month before the phone rang. 'You got twenty-four hours, get ready. You'll get a call at seven tomorrow night.'

Next night another call came through telling me where to go. The fights were held all over the place. They could be in a factory or an underground car park – anywhere you could get a large group of people together. The punters would get the same message: 'Caesar's fighting tomorrow night. You'll get a phone call telling you where.' There might be eighty or a hundred people in the crowd, sometimes double that – mostly suits and socialites with a smattering of knockabouts. Some of them were very high-profile people, the sort that would raise eyebrows if they were caught out mixing it with the underworld. We even had members of parliament come along.

The organisers would bring in fighters from around Australia and even overseas. Well-known boxers and martial artists. I'd be in trackies and bare feet. You can do a lot more with your feet if you haven't got shoes on. You can stick your toes in your opponent's eye.

There were no weapons, but that was as far as the rules went. It was bare-knuckled, anything goes. Something like the Jean-Claude Van Damme film *Wrong Bet*, or the reality TV show *The Ultimate Fighter*, only ten times more hard-core. You could take a bloke's eye out, hit him in the nuts, jam his nasal bone up into his brain, whatever it took to win the fight. There was no ref to make sure no one died.

The purse was usually around ten to fifteen grand, put up by the Little King and two associates of his. I never knew their names but I knew they were well-known straight businessmen. They'd all be there at the fights and made big money betting on the side. A lot of the bigwigs in the crowd were splashing out some serious cash on their bets, too.

There were always about thirty seats for the heavies and big shots encircling the ring – which was a rope circle on the floor. Everyone else stood. Sometimes you'd see blokes with a bottle of Scotch, but there was no bar. This was just a matter of getting in, having the one to three fights on the card, and getting out.

When I first started I was happy just winning the fifteen-grand purse, but then I saw all this money changing hands on the side and I realised that punting was where the real money was being made. I went to the Little King and asked him if I could bring one of my brothers to make bets on the side like I'd seen the organisers doing.

'All right, you can tell one brother,' he said. 'But you gotta make sure that brother knows that he's not to tell anyone else in your family what's going on.'

So I had a word with Shadow and he promised he

wouldn't tell anyone. He came to the next fight with me and used some of the money I'd won on the earlier fights to bet with. We started making some real money that way. In the early days, I got five to one, because nobody knew anything about me. But after I beat this well-known martial artist from Malaysia the odds shortened. Then I beat a very well-known American former champion. He might have beaten me in a boxing ring, but this wasn't boxing.

I liked the underground fighting because every bloke you went in against would be a top bluer, otherwise he wouldn't have been there. And there was no referee or doctor on standby. You never knew whether you were going to win. Even so, I always went in thinking I would. That's something my old man drummed into me. He'd tell me, 'Always know that you gotta be careful. But never go into a fight thinking that you're going to lose, or thinking that the bloke might be better than ya. Always go in thinking that you're gunna beat the bloke easy.'

So I used to go into the fights thinking, Well, you'll be done in thirty seconds. And sometimes that's all it took. Other times it took a bit longer to drop the bloke, maybe two minutes. If you wanted to kill him, that took thirty seconds less.

Once the fight was over, everyone would collect their bets and disappear.

ONE NIGHT me and Snake got a phone call from this sheila Sue. She went out with Mousey, the sergeant-at-arms from the Vikings, and was a really nice sheila, real staunch. She said, 'Can you do us a favour?'

'What?'

'Can you drive me out to Cronulla? There's a bloke out there who has some nine-carat gold cigarette lighters for sale and I wanna buy one for each member of the Vikings for Christmas.'

I thought that was pretty good of her, so I said, 'Yeah, we'll drive you out.'

When we turned up at her place, she had a girlfriend with her.

'Who's this?' Snake asked.

'This is Joanne, Little Billy's old lady.'

'Who's Little Billy?' Snake asked.

'He's a member of the Executioners.'

'Yeah, all right.' So we drove Sue and Joanne out to Cronulla.

When we returned, Joanne's old man, Little Billy, was waiting. With a name like Little Billy, we'd expected him to be some gigantic bloke, but he actually turned out to be a little fella. He grabbed Joanne and started carrying on at us. 'Whaddya doing takin' me old lady out?'

Without missing a beat Snake's just gone, *whack*. Knocked him flat on his back, teeth scattering. 'Now you crawl over here and kiss my foot,' Snake said.

Little Billy crawled over and kissed Snake's foot. Snake turned to Joanne. 'Well, we'll be seein' ya.'

'All right. See ya.'

I rang Sue the following week, after Christmas, to see how the cigarette lighters had gone down.

'Oh, not as well as I thought,' she said.

'Why not?'

'Mousey didn't like it.' I could hear in her voice that something was wrong.

'Hang on,' I said. 'I'm coming over.' I hopped on the bike and rode over to her place. There she was with this big black eye and a swollen lip that was just going down.

'How come you got them?' I asked.

'Mousey got the shits that I let you and Snake drive me out to Cronulla.'

'Didn't you explain you were getting Christmas presents for all the blokes in his club?'

'Yeah, but you know how he feels about you.' He always thought there was something going on between me and Sue, which there wasn't.

I waited for Mousey to get home from work and when he walked in the door I said, 'Did you bash her because she went out to Cronulla with me?'

'Oh no, Ceese, no, no. It was just an argument.'

'Well this is just an argument.' *Whack*. I kicked the shit out of him. I made him crawl over to Sue and said, 'Unless she asks me to stop, I'm gunna keep kickin' the shit outta you.' He was begging her to get me to stop stomping on him. She looked down at him and a big smile came across her face. 'All right, Mousey. Caesar, don't hurt him any more.'

I leant over and grabbed him by the hair. 'You ever lay a hand on her again and I'll be back to finish you off. You'll be going for a ride you won't like.' He knew exactly what I meant because I used to do other work – you know, taking people on holidays that they didn't find their way back from.

* * *

41

SHADOW WAS driving a mate home through Summer Hill one night when his mate said, 'Shadow, pull over. I wanna take a leak.'

So Shadow pulled over and the mate hopped out.

In fact, his mate didn't need to take a leak, he'd actually seen this bloke walking down the street with a case of beer. He grabbed the beer, pushed the bloke over and jumped back in Shadow's car.

Shadow drove off but the bloke got the licence plate number. When the cops turned up at Shadow's place they charged him with assault and robbery. The coppers said to him, 'We know there was another bloke with you. Give us his name and we'll go easy on you.'

'Get fucked. I dunno what you're talking about.'

So he did some time in Goulburn and Emu Plains.

A few days before Shadow was due out, we got on the phone to Sue and tracked down her girlfriend Joanne who we'd driven to Cronulla. We went and picked her up, along with two other sheilas, little Anne and Julie, who had the biggest tits you've ever seen, and took them back to Mum's. We wanted to give Shadow a warm welcome-home gift.

Mum said, 'I know what youse boys are up to. One of these girls is for Shadow, isn't she?'

'They might all be for Shadow, Mum.'

We hid them in a bedroom awaiting Shadow's return.

Shadow walked in the door and first thing he did was go up to Mum and give her a big cuddle and a kiss on each cheek. Then he sat down on the lounge with her to have a catch-up, his arm around Mum. Everyone in our family thinks the world of our mum. All us brothers would die for her. She's a remarkable woman.

Mum and Shadow spent half an hour or so together, but Mum knew we had these three sheilas in the house, so we finally brought them out and said to Shadow, 'Take your pick – or take all of 'em.'

He walked along the line, spotted Joanne and took her off into the bedroom. After that it was on. They were always together. She became his old lady and they went on to have a couple of kids together.

SHADOW MIGHT have had things sorted, but things were a lot more complicated for me where women were concerned.

I was sitting in my booth at the Illinois Hotel at Five Dock – the last booth on the left as you walked into the lounge. My back to the corner. Anywhere I went – the pub, someone else's clubhouse, even my own clubhouse – I always sat with my back into the corner so no one could walk up behind me.

This sheila come up to me and said, 'Nice bike out there.'

'Yeah.'

'Would you like to take me for a ride?'

'Not particularly.'

'If you take me for a ride we can go back to me flat and I'll give you a fuck.'

'No thanks.'

'Well you're gunna regret this.'

'Really?'

'Yeah. I know Caesar from the Gladiators. He's a really good friend of mine, and I'm gunna get him to punch your head in.'

I was taken aback for a moment. 'Really?'

'Yep.'

'Just how well do you know Caesar from the Gladiators?' I asked her.

'Real well. We used to go out together.'

'Well if you know him that well, you should know who I am.'

She looked at me with a blank look and, in the pause, the old barmaid Gladys came trotting over. 'Caesar, there's a phone call for you.'

This sheila looked at me, went bright red, and *whooshka*, was out the door. Old Gladys chuckled, 'I thought you mighta needed a hand.'

Bikers get a lot of women chasing them. When you pull up at a pub, you've got women. When the pub closes, you have sheilas lining up outside. The blokes get on their bikes, point to one of the sheilas, then point to the back of the bike. The sheila trots over and hops on.

Of course I was married, but there was nothing between me and Irene; I really only went home to see the kids. And as it turned out, Irene didn't respect the marriage at all. Around this time I found out she'd been playing up on me with three different men.

I told Irene that as far as I was concerned the marriage was over, and that if I ever caught her cheating on me again I'd give her a real good hiding. For a while I took out this real stunner, Cheree, but I stayed with Irene. I figured that while the kids were young it was my place to be there for them, and I was.

Well Irene was one of these sheilas that just wouldn't listen. She thought more of going out with these blokes than she did of her kids and me, and before long there was a fourth bloke.

I ended up in court when the bloke turned up in hospital and had to have his spleen removed. He reckoned I'd attacked him and the coppers had a couple of witnesses to say that I did. Fortunately the witnesses changed their minds, and then for some reason when the arresting officer took the stand he came up with a new angle: 'On the same day of the alleged assault, the victim was up on the roof of his house cleaning gutters and fell off his roof.'

So they called the doctor back up and the judge quizzed him. 'You've said that the only way this spleen could have been injured was by being kicked in the stomach. Would falling off a roof have caused the same damage?'

The doctor looked at me, then turned to the judge and said, 'Yes, your honour, falling off a roof could definitely cause the spleen to rupture.'

The judge found the charge proven but recorded no conviction. It was the only time I'd ever been to court, and I kept my record clean.

Outside the court the copper came up to me and told me that one of his best mates in the force had the same thing happen to him; his missus had played up with a couple of blokes behind his back. He said, 'I thought you deserved a fair shake.' So there are some decent coppers out there. We shook hands and I returned to the unhappiness of the marital home.

AT THE beginning of May 1978, I was at the Croydon pub, nursing an orange juice and enjoying the spectacle of two good sorts playing pool. One of the sheilas lost the game with all seven balls still on the table, which according to house rules meant she had to flash her tits. So she got up on the table and took her top off. She had big tits, too. But it was the other sheila who'd really caught my eye. As soon as I saw the slender blonde bending over the table, everything stood up. I went as stiff as a board. I knew then that I'd be with her one day. If I hadn't been married I'd have been straight over and asking her out. As it was I had to settle with buying her a drink and talking into the night. Her name was Donna and she was a gorgeous twenty-two-year-old nurse who worked at Camperdown Children's Hospital.

About a week later Irene met Donna, and went out of her way to make sure they became girlfriends. She invited Donna to the movies, made sure she came over for tea. Donna started spending more and more time with our family, until one day Irene suggested that she move in with us.

I was a bit taken aback. 'We don't have the room,' I said.

'Well she can sleep in with us,' Irene said.

So Donna moved in and night after night the three of us would crawl into bed together. Nothing happened, but it was becoming more and more obvious that Irene was trying to push me and Donna together. Irene would sleep on the edge of the bed and more or less turn her back and nudge me towards Donna. Not that she needed to push too hard. It was taking all the strength I had to resist. Maybe Irene was trying to ease her own conscience. Or maybe she thought if I was interested in Donna I wouldn't be watching her so closely and she could play up as much as she liked.

For a long while Donna and I just talked, and we really clicked. I'd never had that with anyone else before. Neither had she. She'd been living with her mum and dad and had only been with three men before. Very quickly she became my best friend, and a few months later, my lover. Once that happened, there was no going back. I knew I'd found the one I wanted to spend the rest of me life with. I could trust Donna, I'd take a bullet for her in a heartbeat. She was loyal, loving, passionate and, above all, truthful. And of course, she was mind-blowingly sexy. But even if we could never have sex again, that wouldn't have changed our relationship. I'd love her just as much. Simply having Donna sitting in the same room gave me pleasure and comfort.

Once it became clear how serious things were between us I said to Donna, 'You wanna think this right through, because being the old lady and wife of an outlaw biker isn't an easy thing, and especially with me. There's a lot of people out there who, for some unknown reason, figure that the way to prove themselves or get a reputation is to either beat me up or take me out. There'll be good times, but there'll be a lotta hard times.'

And the woman said, 'Well I wanna be with you, and the one thing I want is to be your wife.'

I promised Donna that one day we'd get hitched.

Of course Irene was still in the picture, and with the three of us living under one roof, it amazed some people that I had two 'wives'. They didn't know that my marriage to Irene was dead, and that if Donna hadn't come along and I'd stayed with Irene I probably would've ended up killing her. Or at least waited until the kids got a bit older and then left with whichever kids wanted to come with me. Now that things had changed it was time for Donna and I to move out on our own. We got a little place together, and each afternoon I'd go and visit the kids when they got home from school. Then I'd be home by seven for tea with Donna.

A LOT of people think that bikers don't look after their old ladies, but nothing could be further from the truth. I reckon we look after our old ladies better than the normal straight bloke does.

Soon after Donna and I got together, I heard that the sergeant-at-arms of the Phoenix had said a few things about her that he shouldn't have. The Phoenix was drinking in at the Bat and Ball on Cleveland Street, Redfern, so I went in there one night with Donna and fronted the head blokes. It turned out the sergeant wasn't there but me and the other blokes had words. One of them said to me, 'You know we could stomp ya.'

'Okay, go ahead and try.' There were about twenty of them counting their hangers-on, and I had a cracked arm at the time, but I still outnumbered them. After about ten minutes every one of those blokes wearing a Phoenix patch had apologised to Donna. They even told me where their sergeant was. Turns out he was in Canterbury Hospital with a busted leg.

Next day, I headed over to Canterbury Hospital and found the ward this bloke was in. As soon as I walked in he started up: 'I know what you're here for, but I didn't say it. It's just people trying to get me in trouble.'

By the time I left, his leg would've been a lot sorer, and it wasn't the only thing that was broken. He would have had a lot of trouble breathing through his nose, too.

No one speaks disrespectfully of my old lady.

CHAPTER 3

An outlaw club called the Assassins had started up in
Summer Hill, one suburb to the east of our territory, and before long they were prancing around in our
terrain.

We had a meeting and decided that we'd front them
at their pub and give them the chance to move out of
our area. If they didn't go along with it, we'd take their
colours and close them down then and there.

So we headed over to the Summer Hill Hotel. There
were about fifteen bikes out the front so we knew there
was a fair few of them inside, against seven of us. We went
into the old tiled pub and found the Assassins' president at
the long front bar. We told him what the go was. He went
away and had a word with some of his blokes, then came
back and said, 'We'll think about it.'

That wasn't the answer we'd been looking for. I looked
at Bull, he looked at Snake, and *bang*, it was on. I threw

the first punch right at their president. We chased them round the pub. Chop latched onto their sergeant-at-arms with his teeth and had hold of him by the side of the face. Some of them were using chairs to try and hold us off, some had jumped over the bar. When you get into an all-in blue, you pick up the closest thing, whether it be a glass or a chair or a pool cue, and do whatever you have to do to win. If you're a real outlaw biker, you're not doing it for yourself, you're doing it for your club and the blokes that are with you. In a really staunch club, the blokes are that tight, they'd rather cop a hit than let their brother standing alongside them cop it.

It lasted about eight or nine minutes. We knocked them all down and as each of them went down Schultz came along behind us and took their colours. And that was the end of the Assassins.

That sort of thing happened quite a lot – clubs closing down other clubs. Usually it would be an all-in brawl, but sometimes there wasn't even a fight. In one incident at Granville, one club just walked into another club's pub, fronted the president and told him to get his blokes to drop their colours. And they did. Just dropped their colours without a punch being thrown, from what I was told. They'd obviously sussed out the other club and decided they weren't going to match up. But to me, if I had a bloke in my club hand over his colours instead of copping a kicking, he'd be gone. He'd be out of the club and *I'd* give him the kicking.

Another decent-sized club, Salem's Witches, who had the area between Summer Hill and Dulwich Hill for a couple of years, one day just disappeared off the scene. They were there one minute and gone the next. No more

Salem's Witches. Same with the Phantom Lords. They were pretty well known, but same thing. One day they just disappeared.

WE WERE out one night in the southern suburbs looking to even up with some blokes who'd been into Bull. We couldn't find them so were heading home to Ashfield when we stopped at a set of lights and Bull said, 'Next pub we come to we'll go in for a beer.' So coming off Tom Ugly's Bridge at Blakehurst, we turned into the Seabreeze Hotel.

As we pulled in I could see another lot of bikes belonging to a club called the Hangmen in the car park. Oh shit, I thought. My brothers didn't go out looking for fights, but they wouldn't back away from one if you paid them. And it didn't take much to stir them up, especially if it involved another club. All you had to do was stare at Snake and it'd be on.

We went into the pub and the blokes ordered their beers. I got my lemon squash. I never got on the piss. One of the Hangmen came over and said, 'We drink here.'

Shadow came round from the back and said, 'Yeah, so what?'

'Well,' this Hangman said, 'it'd be the right thing to ask us beforehand if you could have a drink in here.'

I could see what was coming. Next thing Shadow's gone *whack*, and hit this bloke. Then Chop and Wack have gone flying through to another part of the pub, and there was a blue going on there. It was all over the place. Before I knew it Bull and Snake were walking out with colours hanging off their arms. They'd closed down the Hangmen.

Bull, Shadow and Snake all carried ockie straps on the backs of their bikes, so they strapped the colours on and when we got back to the clubhouse they went out to the backyard and burnt them.

Once a biker lost his colours he could either go to another club or become an independent rider. Sometimes if there was a bloke in the club that you were closing down who stood up to you and really gave it a go, you might even offer him a spot as a nominee in your club.

The other option for a biker who'd lost his club was to go to a social club or a Christian club. There were a lot of those around. They had the vests and a lot of their blokes looked like bikers with tattoos and long hair. Some of the Christian and social clubs wore colours. Some even acted like they were outlaw clubs until an actual outlaw club rocked up. Then all of a sudden they were a social club. It was an unwritten rule with outlaw clubs that you didn't bash anyone in a social club, and ninety-nine per cent of outlaw clubs left the Christian clubs alone too. Unless of course they started putting shit on your colours or having a go at one of your members – then you'd bash them like anyone else.

A CLUB called the Undertakers had taken to riding around our area. At first they were just drinking at their own pub in Belfield, a couple of kilometres away from Ashfield. That didn't worry us too much, but then they started coming in and drinking at the Croydon pub. We had a word with a few of their members, but instead of doing the right thing, they told us where to go. Which didn't go down real well.

It became like the fox and the hound. They knew we were looking for them so they stopped going to pubs. They'd ride around the area, then dart back to their clubhouse. It took us about two months to track them down.

We rocked up at their clubhouse on a Thursday, their meeting night, kicked in the front door and beat up a few of them. They just threw their colours on the floor.

We'd developed a pretty fearsome reputation. We weren't just a club, the bulk of us were brothers, which meant we had a stronger bond than most clubs. Any one of us would step in front of a bloke with a pool cue and take the hit that another brother was going to cop. When you've got a club that thinks that much of each other, you're pretty hard to beat.

WE'D HEARD about a new club that was hanging round Parramatta called the Comancheros. We'd see them now and again when we were out on rides, parked on the side of the road or in a garage getting fuel.

A mate of mine, Roach, from the Phoenix used to drink with us up at the Ashfield Tavern, and one night he brought in a bloke from the Comancheros, John Boy. John Boy was wearing his colours, which wouldn't normally go down real well in another club's pub, but he was on his own and Roach told me he was a good bloke, so I let him stay.

Roach had hit the road by the time I left my lemon squash at the bar and went to have a leak. John Boy came in after me and told me about the blokes trying to steal my bike.

That's the night I flattened the two blokes and John Boy helped me with the third. That was good of him, because we hardly knew each other. I remember the look on his face when I souvenired the trio of little fingers. I had about twenty-six fingers in the jar by then. I was grateful because he'd helped save my bike and so I'd made that promise: 'If there's ever anything I can do for ya, you got me word I'll do it.'

Little did I know what that promise to John Boy would set in train, and would one day end up costing me.

Towards the end of the seventies we started hanging round a pub called the James Craig Tavern, attached to the new shopping centre that had been built at Birkenhead Point. We used to park our bikes on level two of the parking station, right outside the double doors that led into the nightclub part of the tavern, so we could keep an eye on them while we were inside. The staff would always save us two or three tables right in front of the doors. We'd come with our old ladies and listen to bands like Ol' 55 and Sherbet. I was friends with one of the waitresses, Victoria, and she'd bring us big trays of leftovers from the buffet, cold roast beef or pork and baked potatoes.

We were up there one night and one of the bouncers came up to Bull, who was our sergeant-at-arms. 'There's another bike club downstairs causing some trouble.'

'Who?' Bull asked.

'The Comanchees.'

The Comanchees? Bull looked at me but I'd never heard of them, so we headed downstairs. It turned out to be the Comancheros. One of their blokes was jumping up and down on a pool table.

Bull told him to get off.

'What are ya gunna do if I don't?'

'I'll put ya through the fuckin' window,' Bull said.

He got off.

John Boy was there, and came in from outside. 'G'day Caesar.'

'Ah, John Boy, what are youse doing here?'

'We thought we'd pop in for a drink.'

'Well you know the rules,' I said. 'You should've asked.'

'Yeah, fuck off,' said Bull.

'Calm down,' I said. By this stage Shadow and Schultz and some of our other blokes had wandered in and I didn't want to see a blue.

'Yeah, fair enough,' said John Boy. So he got his blokes and left.

Despite the rough introduction, we began hanging round with John Boy and got to know some of the other Comancheros. One night John Boy brought some of them up to the Croydon Hotel. That night the place was full of footballers, blokes from Wests and Canterbury, and John Boy got into a blue with one of the locals. I ended up facing off against Canterbury second-rower Greg Cook. He was mouthing off about what he was going to do to me.

'Well, come on and do it,' I said.

But his mates came out and told him, 'We're not gunna back you against these blokes,' so all of a sudden he was backing down the footpath. 'I don't want any trouble, mate.'

See, footy players will get in and throw a few punches, put the boot in here and there, but when you take on an outlaw club, you're taking on blokes that have been stabbed, hit over the head with baseball bats and bricks, had glasses shoved in their face, had five or six blokes kick the shit out of them, and they've still got up to carry on. So to an outlaw biker, a fight against a bunch of footballers is nothing. The footy players soon learnt that, because they were standing there like Mr Goody-Goody with their fists up and all of a sudden there was a bunch of blokes standing in front of them with broken glasses and broken pool cues.

The footy players headed for the door, but unfortunately John Boy had been glassed in the hand by this big red-headed bloke. The blood was pissing out and we couldn't stop the bleeding so me and two of the Comancheros got him up to emergency at Western Suburbs Hospital.

They stitched him up and gave him a few shots, but we could hear the sirens coming so we grabbed John Boy and got out of there.

As I GOT to know John Boy and the Comancheros better, they started inviting me over to their pub on Victoria Road, Ermington. It's not a small thing for one club to invite another club member to drink with them – especially as I would rock up in my Gladiator colours. Then, after three or four visits to their pub, I was even more surprised when John Boy invited me to a Comanchero club party. Apparently it was a first for them.

The Comos didn't have a clubhouse, so the party was at a member's house, on the corner of Liverpool Road and Frederick Street in Ashfield. John Boy filled me in on a few things beforehand. 'When you meet the club, don't go off the deep end if you get snubbed by one of our members, Snoddy. He's a bit standoffish. That's just Snoddy, but I know what you're like, and I don't want a punch-up going on soon as you walk in the door.'

As usual I rode in wearing my colours. There were a dozen or so Comos there, and, as it turned out, the first one over besides John Boy was Snoddy. He walked straight up and put out his hand: 'I've heard a lot about you.' We shook hands and spent the next half-hour looking over each other's bikes. Snoddy was a quiet bloke, but intense. I met a few of their nominees, too. My mate Roach was there, having left the Phoenix to join the Comos. Then John Boy came over and said, 'Jock wants to talk to you.' Jock was William 'Jock' Ross, the famously militaristic president of the Comancheros.

John Boy took me into the garage and introduced me to the thick-set bloke with a hard Glaswegian brogue and Coke-bottle glasses magnifying his ice-blue eyes. Jock told me about his life in the army and how he used to be a sergeant in the SAS. Hard-core stories of being dropped behind the lines in Malaya, and cutting off people's heads. He told me he was a black belt in karate and that he had books on Napoleon, Hitler and Genghis

Khan. His favourite was Sun Tzu's *The Art of War*. He said he hadn't wanted to leave the SAS but his captain gave him orders that he thought endangered his men. He belted the captain and got kicked out of the army. He also told me how tight the club was; there were only thirteen of them and they were real close.

We spent about an hour talking. I had to admit he had some staunch blokes in the club, some good bluers, and they did seem to be a close club. But I suspected Jock might be the type who could only talk a good fight.

THE GLADIATORS were going great guns, but building the club up was near impossible with my brothers enforcing the rule that any new nominees had to be able to fight. We'd got up to twelve members but I couldn't see it going any further. We were at the Venus Room one night and we had this nominee called Turk. He was a bouncer from the Texas Tavern and he had a glass eye. This night he was giving Bull a bit of cheek, so Bull put it on him and went *whack*. Well Turk's eye popped out, flew across the bar and rolled onto the floor. With the dim lighting, the eye lying on the floor looked real. Two sheilas were standing there and one of them fainted. Then Bull went and stepped on the eye and shattered it. The second sheila fainted. Cracked her head on the bar on the way down. People were disappearing, pouring out the door. They thought we were going to kill everyone in the place.

The bloke who ran the Venus Room said, 'Can't youse do things outside?'

'Ahhh, give us a beer,' Bull said. So he gave Bull a beer. Bull went back to drinking and then turned to

Turk. 'All right, hand in your nominee badge.' Turk went up to the end of the bar, got a knife and cut the badge off his vest.

At the next club meeting I said to Scultz, Lurch and my brothers, 'This can't go on. The club's never gunna grow if we're gunna make it that to get in everyone's gotta be able to fight as well as youse can fight. Being a good fighter is a big help in a bike club, but it's not the be-all and end-all. You've gotta have blokes who can work on a bike, you've gotta have a bloke who can wire a bike, a bloke who can spray-paint a bike.

'I know what youse are getting at. Youse figure that if you can fight – and really fight – you're gunna have blokes that won't run away when the going gets tough. But to me, that's the wrong way to think about it, cos I've seen blokes who've been really top bluers and as soon as they've copped a few good smacks in the mouth they've chucked it in. Yet you can have blokes who can't fight real well but who'll stay there to the end and cop a hiding no matter what. To me, they're the tougher bloke.'

In a fight, our blokes were worth thirty or forty normal blokes, but I tried to get it into their heads that fighting was just a skill. 'Put it this way, if you went up against a professional tennis player, you'd get your arse wiped. But that doesn't mean that the tennis player is a better bloke than you, it just means that he can play tennis better. And you could turn round and kick the shit out of him.'

But they threw it back at me that we didn't need more people. 'If you got the quality you don't need the numbers,' they said.

'But it's not about numbers, it's about the club continuing,' I argued. 'You mightn't be in the club in twelve months' time. If it keeps dropping down, who's gunna take your place?'

The meeting ended but not the argument. We continued to debate the issue meeting after meeting.

WE WERE down at Bull's place on the Hume Highway at Ashfield and we had a nominee by the name of Mad Dog. Bull, Shadow and Snake had known him for years before the club started, but when he came round I said, 'There's no way he's ever gunna make it as a member.' I'd seen him in blues and he'd go running round and hide behind Bull or Snake or myself. He was one of these blokes that joined clubs for the protection of the club, to have the numbers behind him.

'Yeah, but he's a good bloke,' Snake argued.

'All right, he can be a nominee, but he'll never make a member.'

This night, it was about eight-thirty and there was a bottle-o up at Enfield that used to shut at nine-thirty. 'Mad Dog,' Bull ordered, 'go up and get us five cases of beer.'

'How do you expect him to bring back five cases of beer on his bike?' I asked Bull.

'He's a nom,' said Bull. 'He'll find a way.'

So Mad Dog headed off. A bit over an hour later, we heard this dirty great screeching noise coming down the road. Here's Mad Dog with a piece of rope running off the back of his bike dragging an upturned car bonnet behind him with the five cases of beer on it. He'd gone into a car yard near the bottle-o, undone the bonnet of one of the cars, loaded the beer then dragged it all the way down the Hume Highway. Only problem was he'd left a whopping great scratch mark on the road leading straight to Bull's driveway.

We unloaded the beer, then Bull and Mad Dog reloaded the bonnet with bricks and half a sleeper to weigh it down. Mad Dog headed back up the street, through the main shopping centre of Ashfield, over to Summer Hill, and down to the railway line, extending the scratch mark through several suburbs to put any coppers off the scent. Satisfied he'd created enough confusion he retrieved his rope and zotted back to Bull's.

A week later, we were down the Empire Hotel at Annandale and there was a fair-sized bloke in there with a real nice blonde. Mad Dog went up and was trying to crack onto the blonde. The bloke told him to piss off, but Mad Dog looked over at me and Lurch and said something to the bloke. The bloke looked at me and Lurch. You could see he wanted to smash Mad Dog but he wasn't going to take us on. I said to Lurch, 'Let's go and stand round behind the partition where they can't see us.'

So we moved behind the partition, but Mad Dog didn't see us go, and he was still yak-yak-yakking on to this sheila. He turned and said something to the bloke, then looked over his shoulder only to see we'd gone. He hit the toe and was out of the pub.

At the next meeting I said to Bull, 'Mad Dog's just never gunna make it. If youse want him to hang round to do the dirty work, watch the bikes and go for food and that sort of stuff, you're really not doing him a service because he's gunna think he'll eventually get in, and he's never gunna get in.'

My brothers might have been looking for fighters, but one thing I judged people on was that if you picked a fight, you had to back it up. If anyone hanging round the club was the sort of bloke who walked into a pub looking for a fight only because he had the back-up of the rest of the club, I'd get rid of him. Those blokes are nothing but trouble.

I WAS out for a ride when I saw these four blokes pull over an old fella driving an FB Holden. The four blokes were slapping him round the car so I pulled over and started smashing them. One of them got me a beauty in the kidneys with a baseball bat before I managed to drop them all. My back was aching as I turned to the old fella, 'Are you all right?'

He said, 'Bikie scum.'

Nice.

If I'd been wearing a suit the old fella would probably have thought I was the greatest bloke in the world. But because I had my cut-off on and the tatts, and my long hair and bandana, I was the bad guy.

I got back to the bike, and it took a young sheila of about eighteen to help me lift my leg over the bike. That's how bad my back was. When I got home Donna had to come out and help me off the bike. I ended up in the hospital; I was pissing blood, the whole bit.

* * *

FOR FOUR or five weeks, everywhere I went people were telling me that the Hells Angels were looking for me. I was riding down Parramatta Road at Annandale with Donna when I saw some bikes with death heads on them parked outside the Empire Hotel. I'm not one to run from a fight so I pulled in and we went upstairs to the lounge.

There was this big bloke playing pool, his vest slung over a chair. On its back were the words *Hells Angels Sydney*. He put his vest on and introduced himself as Guitar. He knew who I was. We started talking and as usual it turned out only to be rumours of any trouble between our clubs. He brought over five of his brothers and we chatted for about twenty minutes before I left.

A couple of nights later I was sitting at the bar of the James Craig Tavern at Birkenhead Point when Guitar walked through the doors. Bull and Chop grabbed him and were about to punch him when Guitar called out to me. I told them to let him go.

'What are you doing here?' I asked him.

'Me old lady has just started work in the kitchen,' he said.

I got Shadow to hop the bar and go out to the kitchen. Sure enough, Guitar's old lady Joan was working there, so I said, 'That's fair enough, you can come here anytime you want. D'ya want a drink?'

'Yeah, I'll have a Jim Beam,' he said. 'Whadda you want?'

'I'll have a lemon squash,' I said.

'A lemon squash?'

'Yeah,' Shadow piped up. 'Ceese don't drink.'

So I bought Guitar a Jim Beam and he bought me

a lemon squash, and from then on we formed a pretty tight friendship. He started coming to the tavern most nights and we'd go for rides of a weekend. You could see me and Guitar up the Cross together at least twice a week, a Gladiator and a Hells Angel sitting side by side on our bikes, yakking on. He knew just about every sheila in the Cross. They'd be coming past: 'How ya goin', Guitar? How ya goin' Caesar?'

Other blokes would be up there sitting on their Harleys too. Mostly independents who weren't in a club, like Rat and Shotgun Frank. They'd park alongside each other of a Friday and Saturday night and just sit there. Sooner or later a sheila would walk up and ask to go for a ride with one of them. The bloke would take her round the block, then off to a nearby flat they had for a screw. Afterwards he'd drop her back and continue sitting. That was their life. They didn't have to go hunting the women, the women would come up to them.

We were up there one night when Guitar decided to go for a ride up the main drag. He'd been gone fifteen minutes and I was starting to think something might have happened to him. I was just about to kick over the bike and go looking for him but next minute here he was, tearing down the main street of the Cross, and he'd picked up the Dargie Sisters, a singing duo who'd just come off stage at the Manzil Room. They had on the tight leopard-skin catsuits, big boots, big hair, one of them sitting on Guitar's tank and the other one behind him. Guitar was yahooing all the way along the main drag. Did a big U-ey down at Bayswater Road, then back again, four times before finally pulling in to where I was. 'I'm having a good time tonight,' he crowed.

The Hells Angels were the average size of a club at that time, about fifteen strong. They got much bigger later on, but most of the clubs in the seventies were only around twelve to twenty members. It wasn't until the late eighties and early nineties that club chapters started to sprout up everywhere. I reckon twelve to fifteen blokes is a good size for a chapter. You get to be really tight. Me and Guitar used to talk about it a fair bit. He told me about a brawl in the United States between his American brothers and a club called the Breed. More than ninety members of the Breed took on the Angels at a Cleveland motorcycle show. There were only twenty-four Angels, but the Angels kicked the shit out of them. Four dead to one. Which went to show it wasn't all about numbers. It went on the quality of the club.

I WAS out with the Gladiators one night when we picked up a sheila and took her back to Lurch's flat. All the blokes except me went through her. Then Lurch went and fell in love with her.

I said to him, 'She's only a slut. You're mad.'

Two days later we went round to Lurch's and he was gone. He'd packed up with this sheila and taken off. And worse, he'd taken his colours with him. So me and Bull tracked him down to a flat in Enmore. Knocked on the door.

'Yeah?' It was Lurch. Bull kicked in the door. Lurch was standing there and Bull's gone, *bang*, sent him flying across the bed. As he was getting up it was my turn. *Bang*, and he went down again. Lurch could really fight, too, but he was lying on the floor cowering behind his hands: 'I don't want no more.'

I turned round to Bull at the next meeting and said, 'See what happened with Lurch? He's a really good bluer, he was someone that youse accepted as a member in the club, but when he got a bit of a thumping, he chucked it in.'

With our numbers dwindling I could see the club just wasn't going anywhere. Hanging around the Comancheros and the Angels I saw clubs that were growing and moving forward. As tight as we were, and as fearsome a reputation as my brothers had, the Gladiators just didn't have a strong image as a thriving club. I sat back night after night and thought, How can I change the club? To change the club meant I had to change my brothers' minds, but they were dead set in their idea that all members had to be able to fight.

To a point I agreed with them. I liked a small, tight club. I knew it was about quality and not quantity. But I also realised that for a club to keep going, you had to bring in new blood, and younger blood. You had to have all different sorts of people in your club.

At the next meeting I had one last shot at convincing them. But it was no good. They came up with the same old arguments. They weren't willing to change. In fact, they wanted to take it a step further and introduce an initiation test: if a bloke wanted to join the club he had to hang round for a bit, and then he had to pick one of the brothers to fight. If he beat the brother, or even held his own, he could become a nominee.

I could see this was just never going to work. I thought, Blokes aren't gunna want to come to a club where the first thing they're asked to do is get into a blue with a member, especially when it's blokes like my brothers.

At the end of the meeting I turned around and said, 'Well, I'm handing in me colours. Youse can run the club the way youse want.'

A COUPLE of weeks later John Boy approached me. He'd heard that I'd quit the Gladiators and said Jock had sent him to come and see if I'd become a nom for the Comancheros.

'Will you do it for me? Remember, you gave me your word,' he said.

Since going to the pub and their club party I'd got to know a few of the Comos and some of them weren't bad blokes. Snoddy and John Boy and a few of the others seemed really staunch. But, more importantly, I'd given my word. I don't give it very often, but when I do I keep it.

So I said, 'Yeah, all right, I'll join youse.'

Not long afterwards I ran into Guitar and he said, 'I heard you left the Gladiators.'

'Yeah.'

'Any chance you coming over to the Angels?'

'I would've loved to but you're a few weeks too late.'

'Whaddya mean?'

'I'm a nom for the Comancheros.'

'Ah, fuck! I was outta town, I only just heard that you'd left the Gladiators.'

'Well if you'd come and asked me before John Boy I'd have went with ya.'

But it was too late. I owed John Boy and I'd given him my word. I packed away my Gladiators vest and got a new one with the word *Nominee* written on it. And I became a Como.

CHAPTER 4

Jock Ross had started the Comancheros in 1966, naming the club after a John Wayne film of the same name. In the film, the Comancheros were a gang of white renegade whiskey- and gun-runners with a secret Mexican hideout. By the time I joined up in August 1978, Jock Ross's Comancheros were an outlaw motorcycle club of thirteen blokes who owned Parramatta, the heart of Sydney's west. With no clubhouse, the members based themselves at the Ermington Hotel, on the corner of Victoria and Silverwater roads.

I'd gone from being the president of my own club to a lowly nominee. Being a nominee meant you were there to watch, and to do what you were told. You weren't included in meetings, your opinion wasn't taken into account, and you were always on call so that if there was a shitty job that needed doing, you were available to do it. I watched the other noms being sent on bike watch, building fences, mowing lawns for members – but the funny thing was that I wasn't asked to do any of that. I was being treated more like a member. Maybe they were just respecting my previous role with the Gladiators, but I had a sense that there was more to it than that.

ME AND Donna moved into a house on the corner of Frederick Street and Liverpool Road, Ashfield, coincidentally the same house where I'd gone to my first Comanchero party. And late in 1978 I decided it was time to marry her. I was still technically married to Irene, but that didn't stop us from having a club wedding.

We got a bloke from a Christian club in North Parramatta who was a registered cleric, and I told him the story.

'Well,' he said, 'you know it's not going to be a hundred per cent legal.'

'I realise that, but I want the ceremony. I want to make her my wife.'

'All right, I'll do it for you.'

So we had a wedding ceremony at a Comancheros' house, wearing our bike gear, and Donna legally changed her name to Campbell. As far as the club was concerned, that made her my wife. And Donna was the perfect club wife. She understood that the club was for the men and that the old ladies were only guests. She knew that you kept your mouth shut and you didn't ask questions. And she knew the meaning of loyalty. She made friends and earned a lot of respect in the club. At Christmas, if there were any blokes at a loose end, she'd invite them round for dinner with us. It was a tight club where everyone looked out for each other, and she fitted right in.

MOST COMANCHERO nominees had to serve a nine-month minimum to get their colours, but I was patched after six and a half months. The next day, Jock phoned me up and asked me to come round to his place at Pennant Hills.

I put on my brand-new set of black and gold colours with the image of the condor and a broken wagon wheel, and rode out to the Hills district. Jock's old lady Vanessa brought me a glass of Coke. Aside from running the club, Jock owned a truck and a fencing business, which must have been doing well, judging from the size of his house.

Me and Jock were sitting down talking about the club for a while before he got to his point.

'Is there any chance,' he asked, 'of getting your brothers into the club?' Suddenly, I could see why I'd been given an easy ride. Jock wanted the fighting power of the Campbells.

'You might get a couple of 'em,' I said. My brothers had recently closed down the Gladiators and were riding together as independents.

'I don't want a couple,' he said. 'I want all your brothers. I want to have all the Campbells in the Comancheros.'

I went and spoke to Bull, Shadow, Wack, Chop, Snake and Wheels. 'Jock told me he wants you all in the club. He said youse'll have a sweet run through.' Meaning that, like me, their nominee time would be short and easy.

Shadow was the first to agree, then Bull. Once they'd come over, Wack and Chop followed. Snake was a bit harder to convince. He didn't want to be a nominee. So I had a word with Jock and Jock said, 'You tell Snake that all he's gotta do is turn up on club nights and meeting nights. The rest of the time is his.' It wasn't, strictly speaking, within the rules. Pushing a nominee through like that would have got up the noses of other members. But Jock was president and he seemed to do whatever he wanted.

I passed Jock's offer on to Snake and it suited him. He agreed to come over to the Comancheros. The only brother who wouldn't come was Wheels. He just didn't like Jock.

The night the rest of my brothers were patched, Jock had the biggest grin on his face. He'd got what he wanted. Jock knew that having my five brothers in the club was like getting fifty more blokes. They were staunch, and they would do anything to win a fight. The power and reputation of the Campbell brothers suddenly added a whole lot of weight to the Comancheros.

JOCK ROSS was a military man. Even before I joined the Comancheros I'd heard stories of his obsession with war, how he ran the club like an army. His favourite topics of conversation were his time with the SAS and the strategies of leaders like Napoleon and Genghis Khan. The way he'd recruited my brothers was in line with all that. He was building up his own army, and he wanted warriors. As a Scotsman he was well aware of the Campbells' fame as highland warriors.

Jock's military focus was evident in the club rules. There were fourteen rules in the Comanchero charter, which was pretty standard, but within those rules were a whopping fifty or sixty by-laws. All of them written by Jock. And some of them were pretty strange. Like the ban on associating with members of other clubs. Jock's reason for that was that if there was ever a war with a club that you had friends in, you might not be able to bash them or, if he gave the order, kill them. I had plenty of friends in different clubs so that was one rule I didn't plan on keeping.

The other peculiar thing about Jock was that he wasn't much into his bike. In fact, he had night blindness, so me and another member had to ride either side of him and tell him when to turn, or when to brake. Hence when I first joined the Comancheros there wasn't a lot of riding going on. Jock's idea of going out was to go to the same hotel and do the same thing every week. It was always Saturday night at the Ermington Hotel, playing pool. There'd be no runs to different parts of Sydney like we used to do in the Gladiators. I suggested we go to different pubs where they had bands on, and we started riding into places like Newtown and Glebe, up the Cross, into Darlinghurst and Taylor Square. We also started going for runs out to Blacktown and up to Windsor. It was a motorcycle club, after all, and that's what most of the blokes were there for. They enjoyed the ride.

Not everyone, though. Jock's inner circle were more like him, particularly his two lieutenants, Foghorn and Snowy. Both were life members and always seemed to be in Jock's ear.

Snowy was about five eleven, with thin hair and a thin build. He wasn't a bad bike mechanic but I rarely saw him actually riding. Under Jock's rules, if you were a life member you could do as you liked, so if he didn't want to turn up on his bike, he didn't have to. Instead, he'd go everywhere in his ute. This made the Comancheros completely different from any other club, where the bikes were the reason for being.

Then there was Foghorn, a little bloke with big-man syndrome. He was scrawny – couldn't have been more than five eight and sixty kilos if he was lucky – with straggly hair and a little goatee. He walked with a limp and didn't ride his bike much either.

Snowy and Foghorn didn't like it when my brothers and I came into the club. Not only had our arrival made the club a lot stronger, it had also started attracting more people to the Comancheros. The club was growing and you could see Snowy and Foghorn being pushed aside. Before, they'd been the big fish in a small pond, but they were quickly becoming tiddlers in a big pond. They wanted the power and the attention back with them.

ASIDE FROM the petty power squabbles and Jock's military caper, though, the Comancheros were a tight club. There were some tough blokes and, along with my brothers, a couple of good fighters. There was plenty of riding, partying and blueing to be had.

It was the end of the seventies and we were at a concert down at Parramatta Park when a fight broke out among three other outlaw clubs. There was brawling all over the place, and when one of our members, Lard, decided to get stuck into a bloke, things spilt over into our club. Next thing I saw, Jock was getting thumped. It was the first time I'd seen Jock in a fight, and he was losing badly. I went over and smashed his opponent. He went down and then someone else was calling for me. 'Caesar! Caesar!' It was Roach. Three blokes had him down on the ground and were punching the shit out of him. Roach couldn't fight his way out of a paper bag, but he was staunch. He was always right in there, bleeding but giving it a red-hot go. I grabbed a chain with a big padlock on it from the front of someone's bike and walked up behind these blokes. *Whack. Whack. Whack.*

It was the sort of fight that really got you pumped up. You were punching on with your brothers and you could feel your blood turning hot. There was that buzz you got when you were outnumbered and you were fighting together for your club. There were baseball bats, knives, chains, the whole lot, and then someone would yell out the club name. You'd hear it again and could feel your blood getting hotter. You'd start swinging harder and harder.

I'd dropped the three blokes and was helping Roach up when suddenly there were six or seven more blokes charging down the park towards me. As they got near I grabbed Roach by the belt and the shoulder and threw him at their legs like a bowling ball. They tumbled back and I started smashing into them with the padlock and chain. Then someone yelled that the coppers were coming, and in an instant the fight broke up. Members from each club returned to their own little campsites as the cops appeared and started giving everyone a hard time.

We decided we'd hit the road. But while I was rounding up the old ladies I ran into four detectives and they started quizzing me about the club: How many people were in the Comancheros? Who was the president? Who was the sergeant?

'Get fucked.'

Apparently they didn't like my answer because they handcuffed me, and with two Ds gripping my arms, the senior bloke in the safari suit started whacking me in the guts. 'Come on, tell me what I want to know.'

'Get fucked.'

He continued whacking away, until one of the Ds yelled out, 'His club's coming.'

I looked over my shoulder and there were six Comos coming down the park. The senior D gave me one final whack, right in the nuts, before they uncuffed me and went screaming out of the park.

Well, after that whack to the nuts, I saw stars, but I stayed on my feet and managed to walk back to my bike.

I was pretty crook for the next few days. I missed a club meeting. We had a run to Wisemans Ferry coming up the following weekend so Snoddy, who I'd become good mates with since our first meeting at the club party, rang and asked me how I was feeling.

'I'm pissing blood.'

'Just stay there and don't worry about the run,' he said. 'I'll have a word to Jock.'

Next thing I got a call from Jock. 'Caesar, you stay at home, mate. Don't worry about the run.'

The blokes left on the run on the Saturday morning, but come Saturday afternoon I felt weak about not being there. I was all strapped up so I thought, Fuck it. I got my bike out, kicked her over and headed to Wisemans Ferry, about seventy kilometres away.

Halfway there I felt this wet, warm sensation like I'd pissed my pants. I pulled over to find I was bleeding. I took off my shirt and stuffed it down the front of my jeans.

When I turned up at Wisemans Ferry the first one to see me was Shadow. I obviously looked like shit because straightaway he asked me what was wrong. I told him I was bleeding, so the rest of the club gathered round. They were walking into people's backyards and grabbing towels off washing lines. I had towels stuck down the front of my jeans and on the seat of my bike. Shadow and Wack followed me home and put my bike away. I ended up in Western Suburbs Hospital where they told me I had a ruptured groin from where the copper had hit me. I spent the next week in bed.

OUTSIDE OF my brothers, the best bluers in the club were Davo and Sheepskin. Davo was a happy-go-lucky bloke with curly blond hair and a ginger beard who loved riding his bike. Me and him became good mates. Sheepskin had joined the club not long before me so we used to hang round together a fair bit and he'd invite me to his place for tea. I never asked Sheepskin where his nickname came from, but nearly the whole time I knew him he wore a sheepskin vest, so it might've come from that. One day when I was up at Sheepskin's place he went to get something out of a cupboard, and when he opened the door the shelves were just lined with trophy after trophy from karate tournaments. He'd done a lot of martial arts but he was a good street fighter too. That might be why we got on so well together. In fact, all the Campbell brothers were close to Sheepskin. We were similar, too, in that if you pushed us, well, you'd bitten off more than you could chew. Sheepskin was one of these blokes that wouldn't just give you a black eye or break your nose, he'd take out your eye or rip off your ear.

The only thing that me and Sheepskin really disagreed on was the issue of fighting between members. When I joined the Comos and got into my first meeting, I noticed that some of the tougher blokes were standing over the blokes that weren't real good fighters. Basically saying, 'If you don't vote with me, I'll getcha after the meeting and punch your head in.'

When I saw that going on, I put up a rule that no member could fight another member for any reason whatsoever. Hands went up everywhere. The rule got passed. And all of a sudden you saw blokes that hardly said a word at meetings standing up and giving their opinion on things. It worked really well. But Sheepskin didn't like it. He didn't want to stand over people in meetings, but if someone rubbed him up the wrong way he wanted the right to offer that bloke outside. The problem was, Sheepskin was that good a fighter, if he really wanted to punch on with someone, the other bloke would end up in hospital.

So we had to come up with a new way to settle arguments. Even in a tight club, there's going to be blokes that don't get on, or disagree over something. So I stood up at the meeting and said, 'Look, you don't have to respect the bloke, but respect the colours. While he's wearing the same colours as you, you just don't fight. Whoever wants to be in the club the most will call it quits and end the argument.'

It worked. All the time I was with the club there wasn't one member who ever dropped his colours and walked away because of an argument. You'd see members giving each other dirty looks, but then they'd sit back down. It might take three or four months but eventually they'd start talking to each other again.

To this day I've never laid a hand on a person who wears the same colours as me. But the day I get rid of my colours, well, there'll be a few blokes in for a big shock.

WITHIN MONTHS of being patched, I got a phone call from Jock asking me to be his sergeant-at-arms. I didn't want to accept at first. We already had a sergeant-at-arms, Roger, who was a decent bloke, and I was just happy to be a member. I'd made some good friends in Sheepskin, Snoddy and Davo, and was enjoying hanging round with them.

'Nah, thanks anyway,' I told him.

But Jock wasn't going to take no for an answer. I think the main reason that he wanted me as sergeant was because he knew I could fight, and that I didn't care what I did to win. Maybe it was another way to get me and my brothers in tight. Plus he knew I didn't drink or take drugs. His big argument was that the sergeant-at-arms at the time, Roger, liked to hit the bong and have a few drinks. 'You know that at the end of the night, Roger is wasted. He doesn't know what's going on.'

He had a point. Come midnight or one o'clock, Roger would be out of it. But he was just doing what you were there to do, have a good time. And I hadn't seen anyone get hurt while he was sergeant.

So I repeated my answer to Jock: 'Nah, I'll just stay a member.'

We went back and forth for four hours. Finally I said, 'How 'bout if you keep Roger as sergeant and I'll be his offsider?'

'No, you can't have a sergeant and an offsider,' he said. 'I'll tell you what I'll do, I'll make Roger master sergeant, and you sergeant.'

'All right,' I agreed.

Roger was still considered the top sergeant, and when it was announced, he was the first one up to congratulate me. Turned out he actually was in favour of it, because it meant he could start his partying earlier, knowing that I'd stay sober.

Being sergeant of the club always meant, to me, that it was my job to look after the club and its members, to make sure that nothing ever happened to them, or to the club. I made it a point to let every member and nom know that if they ever had a problem, they could always ring me. Which a lot of them did.

I'd also check out the nominees. I'd get a bloke's name, his licence number, his home address. Where he went to school. I'd want to know who his mum and dad were, where they lived. If he had brothers and sisters, where they lived. I'd check it all out to make sure we weren't getting a copper in the club.

Another part of my job as sergeant was to scope out any hotel we were planning to visit. During the week

I'd check out the entrances and exits, see how many bouncers they had on and what the go was with the manager. Some pubs didn't allow bike clubs, so I'd have a word with them and check it'd be okay if we rocked up on the Saturday night. I'd also figure out the different ways you could get to and from the hotel in case the cops turned up. Anything that would make it easier if there was a problem on the night.

Then, when we actually arrived at a pub, the first thing I did was suss everyone out. I'd look round and see who was doing what. The bloke who was just sitting there taking everything in, who didn't seem worried that a bunch of bikers had just walked in, he was the bloke that I knew would cause us trouble if something started.

It was like at the Vicar of Wakefield in Dural, in the semi-rural outskirts of Sydney. When we first started going there it was a pretty rough pub and I fronted the place like I normally did. I picked out this big Pommy bloke called Dave as the head bouncer and went over to have words with him.

'We'll be coming here,' I told him, 'but if your blokes stay away from my blokes, we'll stay away from them. If there's any trouble, come and see me first. Because if you bash any of our blokes we'll have to bash yours.'

It was a big place and they used to get all the top bands up there. We went there for a few weekends and everything was sweet. Me and Dave got on real well. He didn't drink either, so we'd be up there having a lemon squash or an orange juice. Turned out he was the heavyweight champion of the Pommy navy. One night he and his bouncers got into a fight with a bunch of blokes who'd come in. We went in and helped them out, sort of became extra bouncers for the night. We looked after each other.

One night we rocked up there and the American blues-rock band Canned Heat was playing. It was about twenty bucks to get in so I said to Dave, 'Can you get us in for nothing?'

'I'll see what I can do.'

While all the negotiating was going back and forth between Dave and the band's manager, I said to my blokes, 'Now when the manager comes back out to talk to me, you all just walk into the pub. Make sure you got your old ladies with ya.'

So I was talking to the band's manager and all our blokes were going in behind him. Eventually we came to an agreement that we'd only pay ten dollars, but by that time all but one of our blokes was in.

I said to Dave, 'Look, you got me word, there'll be no problems tonight. I'll keep an eye on everyone.' So we were in listening to the band, and everyone was on the dance floor having a great time. I was watching out for Lard and Snake and Big Tony – the blokes most likely to cause trouble. But everyone was just enjoying themselves, and I thought to myself, Oh well, this is gunna go all right.

A lot of blokes in the club used to say to me, 'How can you have a good time when we go to the pub and you don't drink?' This was my good time: watching the rest of the blokes having fun, watching the old ladies out on the dance floor, making sure everyone was okay.

But about half an hour later, Dave came up to me. 'Can I've a word?'

'Sure.'

He led me towards the men's toilets.

'Whaddya doin'?' I asked him.

'Just come and have a look in here.'

I went in, and there was this bloke lying up against the urinal. Blood everywhere, his face battered to a pulp. He'd had a really good flogging.

Oh fuck.

'It must have been one of your blokes,' Dave said, because the bloke lying there was a big fella.

So I went back out to where everyone was dancing and I was checking out the obvious suspects. Big Tony, Snake, Bull, Wack. But they all seemed pretty happy. Then I spotted Lard with this big grin on his face. Aha. I called him up.

'Did you do the bloke in the toilet?'

'Yeah, he pissed on me foot.'

'Well you could have just belted him,' I said. 'You didn't have to smash him.'

'He pissed on me foot!'

'Oh, all right, just try and keep yourself under control for the rest of the night.'

Dave called the ambulance, the cops rocked up and he fed them some story.

'Thanks, Dave. You got me word there'll be no more trouble tonight.'

Soon after Donna came over. 'There's a bloke over here pulling one of the old lady's hair.'

'Who?'

She pointed out a bloke who was about six foot and fourteen stone with shoulder length hair. I said to him, 'Look, mate, can you see how many of us are in here?'

'Yeah?'

I thought, Oh bewdy, one of these. Wanted to be a tough guy to the bikers.

I said, 'Just leave the girls alone.'

'All right, I don't want any trouble.'

Ten minutes went by and Donna was back. 'Ceese, he's still doing it.'

I went back over and grabbed him by the shoulder. 'Fuck off! This is your last warning. Touch one of the girls again and you're gunna end up in hospital.'

But five minutes later Donna was back. This time I went straight over, and started dragging him outside when he turned round and – *whack* – hit me in the mouth. I thought, You cheeky prick. He took a second swipe, and I thought, You're gunna cop a bit here, pal.

I grabbed his long hair and wrapped it around my left hand while I started whacking up into his face with my right. *Whooshka*. Each whack lifted him off the ground. I had him up against this dividing wall. *Bam, bam, bam*. I could hear Donna yelling out to Bull and Snake, 'Stop him! Stop him!'

'Let him have his fun,' Lard said.

'He'll kill him!' screamed Donna.

Whack, whack. Everything was black. I was in the zone.

Suddenly the bloke fell to the floor. I looked down at him and thought, How'd that happen? I still had a strong grip on his hair.

'Look at your hand,' Donna said.

I looked down and there was the bloke's hair, still wrapped around my hand. And still attached to the scalp. I looked back at the bloke slumped on the floor.

Blood was pissing out the top of his head. His face was like jelly.

Dave came over. 'Who's done this?' He looked at me. 'Not you, Caesar?'

I suddenly felt sheepish. 'I couldn't help it. He was molesting the women, and it's my job to look after 'em. I tried, I gave him three chances. I was even leading him out, and the prick hit me. I let that go, and he tried for a second one. I'm not letting that go.'

'Fuck,' said Dave. 'What am I gunna do? Two in one night.'

The ambulance came and got this bloke on the stretcher. He was out cold. The cops rocked up again and I listened to Dave explain it to them. 'There was a bunch of sharpies here, or punk rockers, whatever you call 'em,' he was saying. 'This bloke got into an argument with them and oh, these punk rockers give him a terrible hiding.'

'All right, thanks, mate,' the copper said, and hopped back in his car and drove off.

Dave came over to me. 'Is that the end of it for tonight?'

'I'll get the blokes and we'll go now,' I told him. He'd been a real good bloke to us and I thought, I'm not gunna fuck up his job for him.

'You're welcome back any other night,' he said, 'but I really appreciate you leaving now.'

We were getting on the bikes when I heard a bloke screaming. What now? I looked over and Snoddy's got a knife to this bloke on the ground, trying to scalp him. Chop, Lard and Lout pulled Snoddy off and I asked him what happened.

'The bloke spat on me.'

'Fair enough. Get on your bike, we're going.'

As always, I waited until every member had his bike going and was ready to leave before I started mine.

We spent the rest of the night back at someone's house going over the night's events, and didn't I cop an earful from the blokes. I was always the one telling them not to get into fights, and there I was doing it.

As for the bit of scalp and hair I'd ripped off the bloke's head, Chop took it home and stuck it on the end of his bed. He had it there for months before the stink got too bad.

WITH THE club's numbers increasing, I suggested to Jock that we should set up a clubhouse. It would be a lot better than just hanging out at a pub and then finding someone's house to go back to.

Two of the blokes in the club, Mousey and Sparksy, were renting a two-bedroom fibro house in among the factories of George Street, Granville. I thought it would make a great clubhouse so I had a word with Mousey and Sparksy and they agreed to find another place to live. Then all the blokes got together and we started ripping out the insides of the house to make it bigger. We put in a bar and stuck up posters and photos of members. There was a backyard barbecue area.

At last we had our own clubhouse where we could invite prospective members, hold our meetings and throw parties. It was a step forward for the club and had the added benefit of attracting even more people to the Comancheros.

Three of those new members included the professional boxers, the McElwaine brothers. The first one to come to the club was Mark. When Snake first brought him round he was riding a Ducati and had on the leather pants, the brown leather jacket and the short hair. When he decided he wanted to join the club we told him he'd have to swap his Ducati for a Harley or, at worst, a Triumph. He got the Harley, became a nom for the club, and I nicknamed him Gloves.

We met his brothers Greg and Phil working in at their dad's pub, the Terminus, in Pyrmont. After seeing how Gloves had adapted so well into the club, they decided they wanted to join too. So I nicknamed them Dukes and Knuckles and we welcomed them in as our new brothers.

All three McElwaines were very handy with their fists but Knuckles was one of the best boxers Australia has ever had. He won gold in the middleweight division at the 1978 Edmonton Commonwealth Games and was the Australian middleweight champion for much of the late seventies. My brothers formed a very tight bond with the McElwaine brothers, and the physical combination of the two families provided the Comancheros with an unassailable power among outlaw clubs. It was around this time that people started calling us Campbells 'the Wrecking Crew'.

OUTSIDE THE club, life was still rocking along. Me and Donna were sweet, and in August 1980 she gave birth to our first child, a son we called Daniel. While Donna took care of all the home side of things, I continued working as a collector for the Little King and another bloke up the Cross. I was also still involved in the underground fighting scene, so every few weeks I'd be called up for a fight. It wasn't for the money; I was making enough off the collecting to live. I just liked the fighting.

My training regime was almost a full-time job in itself. I was at the gym six afternoons a week. It was the same routine every day: come in, do the weights, then work on the punching bags (heavy bag and speed bag). Then I'd work on the board – a springboard about four inches thick and wrapped with cord, which you'd punch into. It had some give in it so you didn't break your hand, but it was designed to toughen up your knuckles a lot more than hitting the heavy bag with gloves. I needed that since I was bare-knuckle fighting. The kyite was good for that too. Punching into the baskets of grain really toughened up the hands. My knuckles were always puffed up. Even now in the sunlight you can see all the scarring. They look real weird. I broke quite a few knuckles.

I'd finish off my gym session with some more bag work and a lot of squats, then go home and have a big drink of protein powder with bananas and strawberries mixed in. Donna was cooking me pretty good meals and we'd have tea together. I'd sit back and watch TV for half an hour, wait for the meal to settle, then go out and run for an hour. I'd do the same thing early of a morning: go for a run down the highway then come home and have a shower.

At that stage I was bench pressing 460 pounds. I had a fifty-four-inch chest, which would expand to fifty-seven inches, and twenty-inch arms. So I was pretty solid, and I had the power to go with it. With all the running I had the breath to go on, too. I had over thirty fights under my belt by then and still hadn't lost a bout. The best odds I could get now were six to four on.

Life was good. I was on top of the fighting game, I had my woman, a new baby, and the Comancheros. And the absolute icing on the cake was when we were out riding in a big pack. Ten or fifteen blokes, your brothers around you, and, like the old saying goes, you had the wind in your face and the sun on your back. I'd be all in black. Black jeans, shirt, vest. Black bandana and sunnies. You'd be cruising along and all the straights in the cars would be hanging out the window, drooling. You could see that they'd love to have been on the bike. Sheilas would be driving with their boyfriends and up would come the tops, tits against the windows. We'd have sheilas hanging out the windows: 'Take us for a ride and we'll give you a fuck.' Even when I had Donna on the back.

When we'd slow down to drive through a shopping strip I'd look behind me. Here'd be every bloke and every old lady checking themselves out in the shop windows. It was the only time you could see yourself in a big pack. In those days you didn't have to wear helmets and the sheilas'd be fluffing their hair. They used to love the posing . . . All right, we all did.

In late 1980 we headed out in a big pack on the national run to Molong, north of Orange in central-western New South Wales. Jock decided to make it a pub crawl all the way, so we went down the Bells Line of Road and stopped at the pub at Kurrajong. My brothers and I, plus a few other blokes, decided that we'd head straight to Molong instead to set up camp.

We hit Lithgow and pulled into a servo to get some petrol. As usual, Shadow and Sparksy were trying to crack onto the female attendant. We all filled up and Shadow ended up with the sheila's phone number. Then we continued up the road to Molong, found a track that wound down to the river and picked out the best spot to set up camp. I had to suss out the hotel so I went back into town to have a look around. I found the local copper and told him what the go was; that there'd be no trouble if they left us alone and that I'd look after our blokes. Then I headed back to the campsite and settled in around the fire.

About one o'clock the next morning we heard the familiar rumble of the pack coming down the road. We heard them turn off to come down the track, then heard Jock yelling out to Foghorn and Snowy to head out across the paddock so they'd be the first ones down to the river. (It was the first time I'd seen Snowy on a bike since I'd been in the club.)

Next thing we heard was a lot of screaming and the metallic crunch of bikes pranging. We all went running up the paddock to find everyone off their bikes and crowded around a big hole into which Jock, Snowy and Foghorn had disappeared. The grass was so long they hadn't seen the hole and had ridden straight into it. Once we realised they were all right everyone cracked up. We spent the next hour pulling their bikes out.

Later that night there was a bunch of us sitting round the campfire telling yarns when one of the old ladies, Jackie, fell asleep next to me. She was resting her head on my leg so Jock went off and found her old man, Tonka, who was over in one of the tents having a bong, and brought him back to the campfire. 'Hey, man,' Jock said to Tonka, 'are you gunna let Caesar get away with that?'

'With what?' Tonka asked.

'Look at your old lady, she's laying all over him.'

'Wake up to yourself, Jock,' I said. 'She's asleep. She's just using my leg as a pillow.'

Tonka wasn't fazed. He turned round to Jock and said, 'Hey, I'd trust Caesar with Jackie anytime. I don't know what you're carrying on about.'

It was only a small incident in an otherwise great run, but it was a side of Jock I was starting to see more of, and it was a side I didn't like.

CHAPTER 5

I used to get called out at all hours to help members with their problems. I might get a call at three o'clock in the morning when a bloke had been kicked out of the house because his old lady had found a phone number in his vest. Knuckles was a serial offender. He got caught with numbers by his old lady, Wendy, about five times. He always kept them in his boot. The same boot. I rigged up a story that he was keeping the numbers for me and that it was my sheila on the side; that Knuckles was doing me the favour. She sort of went along with it for a while, but then she called me over one night at the clubhouse and said, 'Nah, there's no way you're cheatin' on Donna. I know he's playin' up.'

I knew it could be a bit hard on some of the sheilas who were new to the biker lifestyle. They might be a nurse or a secretary and get picked up by a Como, never having had anything to do with clubs. They'd join up and wouldn't know what they were getting themselves into. Some of the older members, when they got a new girl-friend, would bring them round to our place and ask Donna to explain how an old lady should act around the club. It was a big show of respect for Donna and she appreciated it. She'd make the new girlfriend a cuppa and spend some time going through the club rules for old ladies.

'The main thing to understand, right,' she'd tell them, 'is that the club belongs to the men. We are being invited along but it's not our club. We're only guests. Even though we might be married to 'em or whatever. You gotta get that into your head. Once you understand that, it'll go a long way to you understanding how the club runs.

'Now when you get to the club, the first thing you gotta do is work out who the proper old ladies are. Because sometimes the men leave their proper old ladies at home and bring in, you know, the odd stray here and there. They might have them tucked away for a couple of months at a time, or it might be just for that night. But you've got to learn to remember which is which and, most important, never to say anything. You can't open your mouth and tell his old lady. That's the hard part on ya.'

As sergeant it was my job to discipline the sheilas as well as the blokes. So if an old lady did something she shouldn't – like telling another member's old lady that she saw such and such down the street with this little blonde – I had to deal with her. If she was new to the club I'd give her a bit of leeway, and maybe just sit her down with Donna for a talking-to. But if she should've known better, I might suspend her for anything from two weeks to six months.

When an old lady got suspended it meant she couldn't come to the clubhouse or any club do. She could still ride with her old man, and if her old man was going to the pub and two members wanted to go with said member, she could go. But if it was ten or fifteen members going to the pub, she wasn't allowed to attend. And she was definitely excluded from club nights and club barbecues.

I had to enforce those sorts of suspensions a few times. We had one member whose old lady turned up one day and got into a blue with him. She was a real feisty little piece, and they both had hold of each other by the hair and were whacking into each other. She ended up tripping her old man and when he fell on the floor she jumped on top of him and started punching the shit out of him. Then he rolled her over and was punching the shit out of her. They rolled out the front door, down the steps, onto the concrete path, and she was back on top, giving it to him. I thought, This is getting really embarrassing here, so I grabbed her round the waist and carried her off. I banned her for six weeks.

There was another incident where the McElwaines' father, Big Bad Bob, was putting on a barbecue for the club one Sunday afternoon at the Terminus. It was a get-together for the blokes, no old ladies. Back in those days he still had the topless barmaids, so this one old lady got it into her head that there were going to be hookers and strippers at the barbecue. She started ringing round all the old ladies spreading the story. Well, blokes were getting home and getting trashed by their old ladies. I was getting phone calls all Sunday night.

I tracked it all back to this one sheila, Jenny, and banned her for six months. It didn't go down well with her old man. He was going to leave the club over it.

'Well if that's all the club means to ya . . .' I said to him. 'Anyway, you know she was in the wrong.'

'Yeah, but cantcha give her a bit of a break?'

'No, that nearly broke up some blokes' marriages.'

Egged on by Jock, the member didn't speak to me much after that, but I tell you, if it had been Donna in the wrong, I'd have banned her for twelve months.

Despite all that, ninety-eight per cent of the old ladies liked the way the club was run and enjoyed the perks that came with it. Whenever we got a new nom to the club I'd explain to his old lady that if her old man was lucky enough to become a member, they would always be looked after. Any time they went out and there was a member of the club there, they would be protected. If anything happened to her bloke, if he got hurt or if they needed money, the club would look after them.

The best example of how a woman should be in an outlaw club was, of course, Donna. She would arrange to have girls' nights on our meeting nights, so that the old ladies would have something to do while we were at the meeting. Most of the old ladies would go round to our place and Donna would put on some videos or music and have food and drinks for the girls.

I remember arriving home from a meeting one night and there were still quite a few old ladies there. I went into the bedroom to let Donna and them carry on, and

I got a phone call from Shadow's old lady, who'd left earlier. She was wondering where Shadow was, because he normally went straight home after a meeting.

'Give it a couple of hours and if you haven't heard nothing then ring me back,' I told her.

Which she did. So I rang the clubhouse but Shadow wasn't there and neither was Chop. Once I heard that, I had a good idea where they'd be. I headed off to Westmead where Shadow and Chop had a garden flat. I pulled up to find Shadow and this sheila standing outside the flat laughing their heads off.

'What's going on?'

'You wouldn't believe me,' Shadow said.

'Try me.'

'Come in here.'

I went inside and there was Chop sitting on the lounge with an icepack down the front of his undies. Shadow told me that not long before I'd arrived, Chop had been in bed screwing this sheila. He wanted to go up her arse but she was too tight so he went into the bathroom and grabbed a jar of Vaseline. He took it into the bedroom, smeared it on his cock and around her arse, and rammed it in. Shadow said you could hear the sheila scream for a mile. Turned out it wasn't Vaseline but Vicks VapoRub. The camphor in it burnt like buggery, literally. He said Chop was running round the bedroom, jumping up and down all over the place. Shadow had to grab the both of them and throw them in a cold shower. They were in there rubbing themselves, the sheila trying to get the Vicks out of her arse. I could hear her still in the shower. Shadow said it was one of the funniest things he'd ever seen.

I cracked up too. Chop was indignant. 'D'ya think it's funny? You oughta try it.'

'I'm not that stupid.'

I told Shadow about his old lady ringing up wanting to know where he was.

'She's really pissing me off, Ceese. If it wasn't for the kids I'd be outta there like a flash.'

'So whaddya want me to tell her?'

'What do you reckon?'

I knew Snoddy was out near my place visiting an old lady of his that he had on the side, so I said, 'What if I ring Snoddy up and tell him that he took you with him to do some business? That way if your old lady checks with him in the morning he'll know.'

'Sounds good to me.'

So I rang Snoddy and told him the go.

'No sweat, Caesar. Anything for you and Shadow.'

When I got home, Donna must have heard me putting the bike away. As usual she was up waiting for me and walked out topless to ask me if I wanted anything to eat.

'A coupla toasted sandwiches would be good,' I said.

I sat down and put on some music while she went out to the kitchen to make my snack, and it struck me how Donna still turned me on just by walking out without her top like she did that morning. With that thought, I was straight into the kitchen, toaster off, picked her up and carried her off into the bedroom.

CHAPTER 6

We were at the McElwaine's pub in inner-city Pyrmont one night when a taxi came round the corner too fast and mounted the gutter, taking out one of our blokes, Sparksy. The impact broke Sparksy's leg, so Snake and Sheepskin gave the taxi driver a good flogging.

The taxi driver got out of there quick smart and the cops turned up looking for the culprits. I rushed Sheepskin and Snake into the ladies' toilets with two of our old ladies. I got the blokes to crouch on the bowls while the two old ladies dropped their pants so that if a cop put his head under the door it'd look like a sheila was on the loo. The cops went through the pub but couldn't find the two blokes described to them.

The copper said to me, 'Look, we can't just let this go.'

I said to him, 'The blokes who did it were two hang-rounds, Monk and Spider.' Just rolled it off the top of my head. Because I always found if a copper had a few brains, he might know you were crapping on, but if you gave him a way out where he looked all right, you didn't have to get into a blue. 'One was riding a red Triumph and the other was riding a green Panhead. Soon as they attacked the taxi driver they hit the toe – even though the taxi driver was in the wrong. Ring St Vincent's Hospital if you want. You'll find out that one of my blokes is up there now with a broken leg.'

'What were their names again?' asked the copper.

'Spider and Monk.'

'And they've gone, have they?'

'Yeah, but if I hear anything about 'em, what's your name?'

He gave me his name and said, 'I'm down at Central.'

'Well I'll give you a ring.'

'Fair enough.' He smirked and rounded up his blokes. I sent mine back into the pub.

Half an hour later about eighty taxis pulled up down the road at the Edinburgh Hotel, which you could see from the Terminus. All these drivers got out of their cabs and were milling around. Jock was saying, 'Let's go down and kill 'em.'

'No, no,' I said. 'I'll go down and talk to 'em.'

'You'll get killed.'

'No I won't.'

So I walked down the middle of the road towards them. And back in them days I had this strut about me, because I didn't care about anyone. I had it in my head that if I was going to get beat up I was going to get beat up. My old man had always said that no matter how good you were there was always someone better out there, it just depended on how long it took you to run into them. But so far I hadn't found the bloke.

So this night I was strutting towards the taxi drivers, but as I got closer they all started jumping in their cabs, banging into each other trying to get away. I wasn't going to get beat up that night.

The funny thing about that was, the next Friday night, me, Shadow and Chop went into the Edinburgh Hotel to meet a couple of sheilas Chop knew. We were yakking on when one of the sheilas said, 'I was here last Saturday night and there was all these cabs pulled up out the front and this huge bikie come walkin' down the street. He kept comin' and comin'. He was the biggest, meanest, ugliest-lookin' thing you've ever seen.'

Chop turned around and slapped her. 'That's my brother you're talkin' about.'

I just thought it was funny. When I told Donna what the sheila said, she thought biggest and meanest sounded right, but not ugliest.

By 1981 I was still considered one of the biggest and meanest in the underground fight scene, too, but after forty-three fights, and at thirty-five years of age, I was almost done. I was getting to the point where I was liking getting hit, and I was dropping my guard. I knew that it was time to stop before I ended up getting knocked on my arse.

Fight number forty-four, my last, also turned out to be my toughest. I rode up to the designated venue, the dilapidated Finger Wharf at Woolloomooloo, in my jeans and leather jacket only to see my opponent arrive in a limo. It turned out he was a German merchant seaman called Wolfgang Gertz who'd fought in America, undefeated, making big dollars.

I changed into my black tracksuit pants and T-shirt. Unusually, I was wearing joggers because we were fighting on an old wooden floor where you'd pick up splinters real easy.

We stood looking at each other while a bloke stood between us holding a hanky in the air. All the suits, socialites and knockabouts crowded in around the edge of the rope circle. The hanky hit the ground and we were into it.

Gertz hit me with some beauties. I hadn't been hit like that before. Just for a second I thought, Ooh, I might have met the bloke to beat me here. But then I thought, No you haven't. And I started getting back into him. I smashed his nose from one side of his face to the other, then he got me a corker in the eye, cracked my ribs. It was an epic fight, lasting maybe seven minutes. I could have gone on, but I could see that he was fucked. He was covered in blood, his eyebrow was hanging down. I finished him off by breaking his arm and hitting him in the throat.

My top lip was split wide open, I had a lump the size of a goose egg on the side of my head, one eye was swollen shut and my ribs felt like they'd been hit with a sledgehammer.

Shadow was helping clean me up when he noticed that all of Gertz's mates had taken off, leaving him there on his own bleeding all over the wharf.

'Let's help him over to the pub,' Shadow said.

We picked him up and took him across to the Rock'n'Roll. Blood was dripping off me into my schooner of lemon squash. Whatever Gertz was drinking had turned red. We took him up to the hospital, after which me and Wolfy became really good mates.

I'd had forty-four fights, won them all and made a lot of money for both me and my employer. The under-ground fight scene exists to this day, but for me, it was over. As for my extracurricular activities after that, well, let's just say my boss kept me in the holiday business. People who upset him were taken for long trips.

And there was always another street blue right around the corner.

MUM PHONED up one night to say Chop was in St Vincent's Hospital at Darlinghurst. I went screaming into town on the bike, pulled up at Mum's house up the Cross and asked her what had happened. She said she didn't know, but that two of my sisters were at the hospital now. I rode straight there and found the casualty department.

There was Chop, the side of his face swollen like an overgrown tomato.

'What happened?'

'I was up the Manzil Room and one of the bouncers there – you know that big Maori they call Grizzly? – he king-hit me while I was sitting at the bar.'

'Righto,' I said, 'leave it to me. D'ya know how long you're gunna be in here for?'

One of the doctors came over and said it'd be two or three days. 'We have to fix up his cheekbone.'

I went home and filled Donna in on what had happened. 'We're going back up the Cross tomorrow night,' I said.

So the next night me and Donna went up to the Manzil Room. I waited outside while she went in and checked out the club. This Grizzly was pretty well known round the Cross. 'Yeah,' she reported back, 'he's in there.'

I waited for him. Eventually he came out and started walking down the adjacent lane. I walked up behind him and let him have it right in the back of the head, the same way he'd king-hit Chop. He went down and I put the boot in, and I mean I really stomped him. Then I pulled out the buck knife, and while he was lying there, blood pissing out his ears, I took the little finger off his right hand.

As I was walking back to the bike a few of his mates came out of the club. 'You're fucked.'

'You wanna try it right now, cunts? Let's go.'

'No, no. We don't want no trouble. We know who you are.'

'Yeah, well when your cocksucking mate comes round tell him that was from Chop. And not to forget it.'

I went back to where Donna was standing with the bike, holding her purse. On nights like this she always had a friend of mine in it, covering my back. Donna was better than having half a dozen blokes with you. You knew you could trust her and she'd never take off, never put you in it. It was like having your wife and your best friend all rolled into one.

* * *

THE COMANCHEROS had grown to over thirty-five members, which in those days made it a big club. Combined with our physical strength, it meant we also had a big reputation. Which only made us more of a target for idiots. You went for a quiet drink and ran into a bunch of dopes who always seemed to think that if they could get over the top of a few outlaw bikers it made them super tough.

This Saturday night we'd gone for a ride with our old ladies over to the Bridge Hotel on Victoria Road, Rozelle. We'd been there for a couple of hours and there was some bloke there with a handful of his mates spouting off that he was the local heavy. I could see what was coming, but before I could get round the other side of the bar to get rid of him a fight broke out. Naturally all the locals joined in, and some of them were pretty heavy-looking. Our bloke, Roger, was right in the middle of it, and one thing I'll give Roger is he'll always have a go.

One Comanchero in, all Comancheros in. So the whole club was charging round trying to get to these idiots. Some climbed the bar and dived onto these six or seven blokes. We didn't even hear the pop. Someone just turned round and said, 'That bloke's got a gun.' And there was this bloke standing there with a gun. One of our blokes grabbed it off him, and we finished kicking the shit out of them. When we were done we got out the front, and I made sure there was no one left inside. Got everyone on their bikes and we left.

We made it as far as Great North Road, heading back towards Five Dock, when I heard someone yelling, 'Pull over! Pull over!' I pulled the pack over and Roger hopped off his bike. He put his hand inside his deck and said, 'I'm bleeding.' Donna, who was a nurse, had a look at it, then me and Sheepskin had a squiz. There was a small hole in his chest on the right-hand side. He'd been shot.

We went back to our place and got Roger on the bed. Sheepskin decided that he was going to play surgeon. He got out some of Donna's nursing gear and was setting up, with Roger yelling out, 'I wanna doctor!' We decided to give the woman a go instead, but when she'd had a proper look she said, 'No, it's too far in. It'll only cause more damage.' So we took Roger up to Western Suburbs Hospital and they took him in to be operated on.

The next morning when I got up there to visit him, Roger said, 'Have a look at this,' and lifted up his gown to show me this dirty great wound, a massive curve of stitches that went all the way from his hip, around his back, and up to his chest. It looked like he'd been bitten by a white pointer, and all from one little .22 slug.

As MUCH as we enjoyed our growing size and reputation, the downside of a big club was that we were starting to lose some of the tightness. Once a club gets big, there are some blokes you hardly even know, and the club fractures into different alliances. This was what started to happen to us, aided in no small part by Jock, who had a habit of encouraging division among members. We still operated as a whole, because we all respected the colours that joined us, but you could see the different groups that were forming. Jock had Snowy and

Foghorn and a few other allies, while I was tight with my brothers, the McElwaines, and blokes like Davo, Roach and Snoddy.

My brothers and I all wore a Campbell ring, a silver shield with a boar's head in the middle, with Campbell written across the top and the wearer's name engraved along the bottom. In 1981, we decided to start a tradition of giving rings to some of our 'brothers' outside the family, to make them honorary Campbells. We had a vote on it and decided the first person to receive a Campbell ring would be Roach.

It was a bit of a funny choice, I suppose, because he wasn't the best fighter going round (even though he thought he was). But he was real staunch. He would never leave you. And to me, that's the toughest sort of bloke.

Snoddy was next up for a Campbell ring. Snoddy had become like family, especially to me and Shadow. He was always round our place. He didn't have his own family. There were stories around about him being an orphan and worse, but I'd seen him close down when other people asked him about it, so I just never asked. I figured if Snoddy wanted to tell me his life story he would.

I wanted to give a Campbell ring to another of our members, Animal, who was tough and staunch and a good bloke, but Jock had gotten into Chop's ear, trying to create divisions the way he did. So Chop vetoed that ring.

Some time later we gave rings to Dukes, Gloves and Knuckles McElwaine. I would have liked to have given Sheepskin one too, but even though we were very good friends, he remained in Jock's camp, so I just couldn't do it. As for Jock, it always pissed him off that he never got a Campbell ring.

One of the youngest blokes in the club, Junior, was another fella who had my respect. He was one of the best members you could have. As a nominee he was always the first up, collecting the firewood on a run or standing his bike watch, and it was the same when he became a member. He would do anything for you. He was a good mechanic and if someone's bike broke down Junior would work on it. He was also one of the best cartoonists and painters you've seen, and was always doing caricatures of the other fellas.

He was a big strong bloke but one thing about Junior was that he could not fight. He was just like Roach, staunch as, but dead set couldn't throw a punch to save himself. So he asked me to teach him.

He started coming to the gym with me to train. I put the gloves on him and tried to teach him to box. He couldn't box. I tried to teach him kickboxing. He couldn't kick. I tried to teach him Muay Thai, judo. He was hopeless. But I'd been in fights where there'd been six, seven, sometimes nine blokes, and the only person with me was Junior. At the end of the fight, I'd have decked most of the blokes, some would have run off, but Junior would still be standing there with his black eyes and a split lip. He was little more than a punching bag but he would never leave me. And I value that more than any flashy fighter.

We certainly had plenty of good men but then there were the others.

***

KRAUT FIRST rocked up to the club in his Holden Commodore with customised numberplates that read *SS*. The plates went with the Nazi swastika armbands and replica ring he wore, and the SS dagger he carried. He was all in black, his pants tucked into his heavy black boots like the Gestapo, with a matching cap. As I watched him walking towards the clubhouse, old war movies were flashing through my brain. I thought, Oh, you gotta be kidding.

Sheepskin introduced him around and when Kraut put out his hand to me, I just looked at him and walked off. Sheepskin wasn't surprised because I don't make friends real easy. I used to meet heaps of people and they'd get insulted. I wasn't really trying to insult them but I can tell if I'm going to like someone just from watching them walk towards me. As soon as I saw Kraut, I thought, I'm gunna hate this bloke.

At first it was the posing, but then I was listening to him talk and when something came up about bikes he said he didn't own a bike; he'd never even ridden one. I thought, Well what are you doing here then? Sheepskin saw me staring and came over: 'You'll get used to him.'

'I don't wanna get used to him.'

Apparently Kraut had been an explosives expert in the army, so Jock was straight up and arm around him. It was a done deal: Kraut bought himself a Triumph and before he could even ride it he became a nominee.

With around forty members by this stage, Jock was in his element. He'd even started referring to the club as his 'army'. Then one night I received a phone call from him and he hit me with his latest idea. He wanted to form a group within the club called the Centurions, and he wanted me to head it up. The Centurions, he said, were to be his own personal bodyguards.

'Who else is gunna be in the Centurions?' I asked.

'Just you and your brothers.'

He said that he'd picked us as the six best fighters in the club – me, Bull, Wack, Snake, Chop and Shadow – and that we would only be answerable to him.

It only took me a minute to decide. I didn't like the idea. It would only cause trouble. I'd already seen the way Jock encouraged arguments between members – like he'd tried to do with me and Tonka at Molong – and I could see what would happen if we formed an elite group within the Comancheros. Jock would be geeing the rest of the blokes up about us, then he'd be telling us what the other members were up to. So I knocked him back.

But Jock wasn't going to be put off the idea of a personal bodyguard. After I turned him down, Jock approached Sheepskin with the same idea. Only this time it wasn't to be called the Centurions, it was to be called the Strike Force. And unlike me, Sheepskin said yes.

So Sheepskin was to be sergeant of the Strike Force, while I remained sergeant of the Comancheros. Jock spelt out that this meant Sheepskin could only tell the Strike Force what to do, and not anyone else in the club, while I could tell the rest of the club what to do, but not the Strike Force. It all seemed a bit stupid to me. If I thought the Strike Force was getting out of line or prancing round the club like their shit didn't stink, I was going to tell them to pull their heads in.

Fortunately, Sheepskin and I remained good mates so I knew I wouldn't get any grief from him.

Jock announced the other members of the Strike Force, who naturally included Foghorn and Snowy, as well as his new best friend Kraut, even though he was still a nom. Then there was Sparra, Tiger, Tonka and JJ. JJ was another bloke I didn't have any time for. As a nominee he was the nicest bloke you could want to meet, but once he got his colours he was a different man. Shadow and I rocked up to his place one day about two weeks after he'd been patched. We could hear all this whimpering coming from out the back. The front door was open so we walked through. JJ had a couple of bull terrier cross cattle dogs, and his bitch had just had pups. When we got out to the backyard, we found this row of tiny pups, only three or four weeks old, nailed through their throats to the fence. JJ was just hammering in the last pup. Shadow lost it. He grabbed JJ and kicked the living shit out of him. 'You can bring me up at the next meeting, but you're the lowest cunt I've ever seen.' I don't think me and Shadow ever spoke a word to JJ again.

And that was the sort of bloke Jock wanted in his Strike Force.

As predicted, the formation of the Strike Force didn't go down well. In fact, it was the start of a whole lot of trouble.

CHAPTER 7

We were at a club meeting one night when Jock announced that he was going to start drilling us for future fights. He said there was an old army manoeuvre where you had one lot of troops at the front line, and a back line that would come in to relieve them. I knew where he'd got it from. It was from back in the days of the old one-shot rifles. You'd have one line of blokes at the front and once they'd fired, the group standing behind them would step forward to fire while the first group reloaded. Jock had reinterpreted this to apply to brawling. He figured we'd have one lot of blokes in the front line who'd take the brunt of the fight, and then a second lot of blokes that would come in to give the first line a breather. He started taking us through regular drills so we could perfect the manoeuvre. He'd stand out the front and raise his hand: 'Forward!' And the front line, full of his best fighters, would step forward. Then he'd point backwards

CAESAR CAMPBELL

and bark: 'Back!' And the front line would part to allow the second line to step through.

It was pathetic. Anyone could see it was just never going to work. It might work if you were fighting in a park or a paddock and you could line everyone up, *and* if the opposition was willing to do the same thing and line their lot up. But in a pub situation? I'd been in that many pub brawls, fighting with my old man since I was twelve, and once a fight started you didn't know where anyone was. People were all over the place. Jock just didn't understand.

As it turned out he never even tried to put it into action. He couldn't. Pub brawls had a life of their own. All that the drills achieved was to reinforce my suspicions about Jock and his military obsession. One Saturday night he walked into the clubhouse and declared, 'El Supremo has arrived. From now on I shall be referred to as the Supreme Commander.' Blokes just looked at each other.

The rest of us, outside the Strike Force, only wanted to ride our bikes, have fun and look after each other. But Jock managed to turn everything into a war game. Like one run we took out to Lithgow. We'd set up a bush camp with a big bonfire, the bikes all parked in tight around the fire. It was a dark night and Jock decided we'd play one of his games with members versus nominees. He put me in charge of the noms. Jock's game had the members going out in the bush to hide, while the nominees defended the bikes. If one member could sneak in and touch a bike, Jock's group won the war. But if we caught the members out before anyone got to a bike, then we won.

116

So the members all went out into the bush. I kept a few noms round the bikes, and sent the rest out just as far as the scrub, so that any member trying to sneak in couldn't see them. One nominee, Pommy, who was considered by everyone to be hopeless, climbed a tree just outside the light from the fire to act as a lookout.

It wasn't long before I heard Pommy's voice: 'You're dead, Jock.'

The nominee considered the worst bloke in the club had taken the first prisoner, and it was El Supremo.

After that we got member after member coming in and we'd tag them. The game dragged on for ages until we heard a strange car coming down the dirt track towards the bonfire. I watched it approach, and as it was coming I could see the boot bouncing a little. So I grabbed a few of the noms. 'When this car pulls up, rip open the boot.'

The car pulled up and it had a straight in it: 'Oh, I saw the fire so I thought I'd drive down.' The nominees ripped up the boot and there were John Boy and Roger. They'd walked all the way up to the road, hailed down the car and conned the bloke into driving down to the campfire with them in the boot. Their plan had been to jump out and touch one of the bikes. Too bad.

After about three hours, there were still four members out in the darkness who hadn't been caught, and weren't going to get caught because they weren't moving, so I declared game over and we got back to the business of partying. All except Jock, who spent the rest of the night pissed off that he was the first prisoner caught.

The other thing Jock tried to do was introduce a compulsory all-black dress code for the club. I always wore black anyway, so that didn't bother me, but he wanted us in the high, black Nazi boots and black helmets with Comanchero colours painted on the side. You didn't even have to wear helmets in those days.

The pathetic thing about Jock's war mentality, though, was that his credentials didn't even back him up. When I'd first met him, and many times since then, we'd sat around tables with him telling his SAS stories of head-chopping derring-do. Turned out it was all crap. One day me and Snoddy were over at his house and Jock's missus, Vanessa, brought out the photo albums of his army days. Here was Jock putting up a fence, here he was building a bridge. Snoddy and I looked at each other. 'What's Jock doing?'

'That was his job in the army,' Vanessa said. 'He was a sapper. An engineer.'

'Not in the SAS?'

'Nah.'

AROUND THIS time we were having trouble with the Warlocks. Someone had said something they shouldn't have at a pub one night and so Jock declared war on them. *One Comanchero in, all Comancheros in.*

It took us a while to track them down because they kept moving from spot to spot. But one night Snowy from the Strike Force came to a meeting and said he'd located the Warlock's clubhouse at Mount Druitt and checked it out.

Jock decided we'd hit them there. Snowy wanted to be the first one in, since he'd found the clubhouse. We all agreed, and Jock decided he would stay out of it since he was too valuable to go on the hit. Evidently anyone else in the club was replaceable.

We sussed out the Warlocks' clubhouse beforehand. It was just an ordinary-looking house, but Snowy assured us it was the real deal. 'Give me the gun,' he demanded.

The hit went down with Snowy in first, armed with a pistol, and Roach as back-up. The rest of us were watching from cars. We saw one of the Warlocks open the front door, and as soon as he saw a couple of Comos standing there he grabbed a sawn-off shotgun. Snowy froze.

Seconds dragged on as we watched Snowy just standing there, not moving. Fortunately Roach pushed Snowy out of the way and dived on the Warlock with the shotty, and we all headed for the house. By the time we got there, Roach was on the ground wrestling with a couple of Warlocks. Our blokes started smashing the shit out of them. It wasn't hard. There was eight of us and only four of them.

We later found out that it wasn't even the Warlocks' clubhouse, just a house belonging to one of their members. We had a rule in the Comos, which I'd brought in, that you never hit a person's home. You could hit a clubhouse, you could hit someone in the street or in the pub, but under no circumstances could you go to their house. You just didn't know if their old lady or kids would be there. I was filthy, as was most of the club. But Jock and the Strike Force regarded the hit on the Warlocks as a great victory.

***

NOT LONG after, we went on a run down to Batemans Bay on the south coast. We met a couple of sheilas down there and most of the club went through them. One member, Lard, became quite friendly with one of them and stayed in contact with her after we'd returned home.

Next thing the rest of us knew, we were at a club meeting and Jock was wanting to go to war with the Rebels.

'What? Whaddya wanna go to war with the Rebels for?'

'I've got my reasons.'

'We can't go to war unless we know the reason.'

After hours of arguing Jock finally told us. It seemed that two weeks after we'd been to Batemans Bay, the Rebels had turned up down there and met the same pair of sheilas. Same thing happened as with us, apparently. They had a good time together. But the sheilas rang Lard and told him that the Rebels had carved into a table:

Comancheros suck
Rebels rule

And that was it. That was Jock's big reason for wanting to declare war.

'You gotta be joking if you wanna go to war for that,' I said.

'We can't let them get away with that,' he said.

'Listen,' I said, 'I'll go and have a word with the president of the Rebels and see what he has to say about it.'

Jock wasn't real happy with this but the rest of the club, barring the Strike Force, voted in favour of it.

So I met the president and sergeant of the Rebels out at Leppington. We discussed the matter and the president told me they'd had trouble with the two sheilas, that it looked like a case of revenge. 'So you want to go to war over a couple of sluts?'

'No, the club doesn't, but Jock does.'

'Why isn't Jock here fronting me himself then? He's your president, isn't he? I'm here as the president of my club, why isn't he?'

'Well I'm the sergeant and this is what I do for the Comos.' Jock didn't believe in meeting with other people.

The president of the Rebels gave me his word that what the sheilas had said was bullshit. We shook hands and at the next club meeting I relayed what had happened. They all voted not to go to war. Jock wasn't real happy about it but he was bound by the vote.

Later on, though, Shadow, Snoddy and me overheard Jock talking to Kraut about dynamite and the Rebels' clubhouse. We fronted them and it came out that, in spite of my mediation talks with the Rebels, Jock had twice sent Kraut to size up the Rebels' clubhouse. He wanted Kraut to work out how much dynamite it would take to blow it up, and was talking about doing it on a meeting night or even a club night, whichever he figured would get the most members. If it had been a club night he would have got old ladies, too. People who were just there to party. But Jock didn't care.

I was filthy. The club had voted for talks, and he'd gone off in secret to do this.

'What are you gunna do?' I asked him. 'Just blow up the clubhouse with 'em all in it?'

'That's the idea,' Kraut piped up.

'I'm not fuckin' talking to you, prick.'

'The Rebels are gettin' too big for their boots,' Jock argued. 'And the Angels will be next.'

'Fuck me roan. D'ya wanna be the only club in Australia?'

'Yeah.'

'Oh jeez, that'd be great fun, wouldn't it.' To me, a big part of being in the club was the dynamic that existed between the various clubs. Not being at war with them, but knowing that if you rode through someone's territory, you might end up with eight or nine bikes chasing you down the road. You'd have to pull over and there'd be an all-in blue. I liked that tension. Often if I had nothing to do I'd pick out some club and spend half an hour riding round their area, or past their clubhouse. Sometimes I ended up in blues, other times I just rode home. But when Jock turned round and said that he wanted to be the only club in Australia, that's when I knew we were in for big troubles. Because it would go from the Warlocks to the Rebels, to the Angels, to whoever was next on his list.

I ROCKED up to the clubhouse one Saturday night and there was Kraut out the front, on his Triumph, with three nominees propping him up. I couldn't work out what was going on so I watched them for a while and couldn't believe what I was seeing: the nominees were literally pushing Kraut around the block. Kraut, a nominee himself, still couldn't ride.

Junior was standing there too, and he seemed really

upset. You didn't see Junior mad often, he was a quiet bloke, so I asked him what was wrong.

'They've just given Kraut his colours,' he said.

'Who?'

'Jock and Sheepskin.'

'They can't do that. It's not even meeting night. You need a hundred per cent vote to patch someone. Fuck, the bloke can't even ride.'

I went inside and asked Jock what was going on.

'Kraut's been given his colours,' he said.

'Whaddya mean Kraut's been given his fuckin' colours?'

'We've just voted on it and he'll be patched at the next meeting.'

'You're fuckin' kiddin'. You're supposed to wait till a meeting to vote on colours.'

'Well as president I have the right to call a meeting whenever I want.'

'Yeah, but there's s'posed to be a hundred per cent attendance.'

'Well the members who were here tonight decided to overrule that and give him his colours.'

'Which members?' I asked, looking into the small shag room off the main area. Standing in there was Jock's Strike Force. They were the ones who'd voted for Kraut to get his colours. 'What about Junior?' I asked. 'Junior was here. Did he vote?'

'Junior wasn't in the room.'

Junior butted in: 'I told you, Jock, that Kraut wasn't to get his colours.' It was the first time I'd ever seen Junior stand up to Jock.

'I don't care what you fuckin' say,' said Jock. 'Kraut's got his colours.'

Sheepskin was standing there but he wouldn't look me in the eye. I just walked out and said, 'You gotta be fuckin' jokin'.'

Kraut was patched at the next meeting. You could have cut the atmosphere with a knife. Normally when a bloke got his colours it was a big party and you had every bloke in the club congratulating the new member. It was a real brotherhood thing. But the only blokes that went near Kraut that night were the Strike Force. The rest of the club didn't want nothing to do with him.

Kraut spent the next month learning to ride his Triumph without someone holding on to him before he was allowed to ride with the club. And on his first run with us, we only made it a couple of kilometres from the clubhouse before he came off and brought down nearly half the pack. Luckily there was only minor damage to a couple of bikes, but I think even Jock was sorry then that he'd given Kraut his colours. On the ride home I pulled him out of the pack and made him ride a hundred yards behind the rest of us. He was just too dangerous.

Kraut was told that he couldn't ride in the pack for at least two months, during which time he had to practise hard. At the end of the two months, Sheepskin and I took him for a test ride down the road. He seemed to handle it so we agreed he could rejoin the pack, but he still had to ride at the back.

No ONE outside the Strike Force was happy about how Kraut got his colours. It really split the club. One night Snoddy was over at my place for tea and we were yakking on about how much the club was changing.

'We've gotten to be the biggest club in Sydney,' Snoddy said. 'We've got some really top blokes. We should be stoked. But there are some real dodgy blokes who've slipped through the cracks, too.'

'It's Jock's attitude,' I said. 'Wanting to go to war with other clubs, and the whole Strike Force. The way he turns people in the club against each other. It's like he only wants to keep people in small groups.'

'Whaddya mean?' Snoddy asked.

'I've heard him telling Bushy that Sheepskin hates him and then heard him telling Sheepskin that Bushy hates him. The whole thing. I've heard him tell Animal how Chop hates him, then turn around and tell Chop that Animal hates him.'

'That doesn't surprise me. That's how he tries to stay in control, keep everyone in little cliques.'

'Yeah, but it's ruining the club. What about the brotherhood?'

'Y'know,' Snoddy said, 'this isn't the first time this has happened.'

'Whaddya mean?'

Snoddy told me there'd been two previous splits in the Comancheros, the last one just a year before I'd joined. He said a bunch of members, led by the former vice-president and sergeant, had left after falling out with Jock.

'What happened?' I asked.

Snoddy said the whole thing started after the former vice-president came up with the innocuous idea of the club holding bike shows. A lot of blokes, including Snoddy, liked the idea, but Jock and his cohort shot it down. With the ute-driving Foghorn and Snowy in his ear, Jock decided to flex his presidential muscle and put an end to the debate by banning bike shows altogether. After that, the vice-president, sergeant and a bunch of other members just left the club.

I'd heard about the former vice-president and sergeant from Jock previously; his version was that they were fuckwits. Especially the former sergeant, a fella by the name of Branko. I remembered one particular story Jock had told me about a night out with the club at some dance in Wentworthville. Jock claimed that this big bouncer had put it on Branko and that Jock had come to Branko's rescue and flattened the bouncer. I told Snoddy the story.

'Have you ever seen Branko?' asked Snoddy.

'No.'

'He doesn't need anyone to look after him. That's just Jock bullshitting.'

Jock had also warned me that since I'd joined the club, Branko had been going round saying he was going to kick the shit out of me. I asked Snoddy if he knew anything about it.

'Dunno about that,' Snoddy said. 'I thought they were good blokes.'

I decided to test just how much of Jock was bullshit. Some time later I tracked Branko down and fronted him. Soon as he realised who I was he wanted to know, 'Whaddya got against me?'

'You're the one who's been running round mouthing off about me,' I said.

'No I haven't,' he said, before it dawned on him. 'Hang on, did Jock tell ya that?'

'Yeah,' I replied.

'Right, you got twenty minutes?'

'Yeah.'

We sat down and he told me about the split in the club; how five or six blokes had just walked out because of Jock. He warned me, 'Don't believe anything he says to ya.'

He said that the incident at Wentworthville had really gone down with Jock getting belted by the big bouncer. Branko, a fair-sized bloke as Snoddy had said, went over and dropped the bouncer. But by the time they got back to the clubhouse it was Jock who'd rescued Branko rather than the other way round. And that's how the story was told from then on. Which, needless to say, Branko didn't appreciate.

IN EARLY 1982, Snoddy and another member, Charlie, went over to the United States to buy some cheap Harleys. Snoddy had arranged with some friends from the Hells Angels that some of their American brothers would meet them at the airport when they arrived in California, then show them around and help them to buy some bikes. But when Snoddy and Charlie turned up in Los Angeles there were no Angels there to meet them. So instead they forked out $400 for an old Dodge and headed off across the States. They ended up in Albuquerque, New Mexico, at a motorcycle shop called Crazy Larry's, where they got talking to some of the local outlaw bikers from a club called the Bandidos. They were one of the biggest outlaw bike clubs in America. When the Bandidos found out Snoddy and Charlie were from Australia they invited them to a local bar to drink with them. The rest of the Albuquerque Bandidos rocked in, including the president, Ha Ha Chuck. They got talking to him and ended up staying at his place for a few days. Ha Ha arranged for some bikes to be brought up from other chapters of the Bandidos, and Snoddy and Charlie had them shipped back to Australia.

When Snoddy got home he couldn't stop talking about the Bandidos and the way they operated. Snoddy said the Bandidos ran things so differently to Jock's military unit. The Bandidos were like an outlaw club was supposed to be. It was old school: honour and loyalty and having a good time with your brothers. Basically a bunch of blokes getting on their bikes, going out and partying. Everywhere there was one Bandido, there'd be another half a dozen Bandidos. According to Snoddy they were like a family. His stories struck a chord with me because that's what I wanted the Comancheros to be. One big family that partied together and looked after each other. Not going out playing toy soldiers.

The rest of the blokes (barring the Strike Force, of course) were as rapt as I was. It pissed Jock off something fierce, because he reckoned the way he ran the Comancheros was the only way to run a club. Snoddy even told Jock, 'If we'd been Bandidos, Kraut would never have got his colours.'

There wasn't a lot we could do to change Jock's style, but one thing we did do in admiration of the Bandidos was stop calling our nominees 'nominees'. The Bandidos called their blokes 'prospects', so we started doing that too. Jock hated it, but I thought it sounded better, and as I was in charge of the prospects at the time, I made an executive decision.

It was only a small step, but it would prove to be a significant one. And I think it dawned on Jock then that things were starting to change.

CHAPTER 8

On 7 February 1982, my mate John Boy, who'd first brought me into the Comancheros, was riding up Woodville Road with Bushy, heading towards Merrylands. He was making a right-hand turn at a green arrow when a car coming in the opposite direction ran the red and hit John Boy dead on. He didn't stand a chance. Any club tension was put aside while we mourned the loss of a good brother and organised his funeral.

It was a traditional club funeral. On the day, we draped John Boy's coffin in a Comancheros banner and placed it on a customised sidecar. Then we began the slow procession up the F3 to Palmdale Lawn Cemetery north of Gosford on the central coast, where we buried our members. There were Comanchero bikes in front of his coffin and Comanchero bikes behind. The old ladies followed in cars, along with more bikes ridden by some Hells Angels and independents who'd known John Boy.

Then there were more cars carrying friends of the club.

At John Boy's graveside, seven members lined up with shotguns which they fired into the air, in the traditional Comanchero seven-gun salute. It made the TV news.

On his headstone we inscribed the words: MAY HE RIDE HIS KNUCKLE FOREVER.

NOT LONG after we lost John Boy, I was up the Cross when I got into a punch-up with a bunch of heavies. A gun came out and I got shot in the side. The bullet hit my hip and embedded itself in my stomach.

I was bleeding heavily so Donna ripped off this soft top she was wearing and whacked it in there to stem the bleeding. All the way home to Ashfield on the bike she was pressing it into the wound. We only just made it.

Back home, Donna got out the scalpel and the tweezers, then started feeling round for the slug. She stuck a probe in the wound but couldn't feel anything so started squeezing and prodding around the rest of my stomach. She reckoned she could feel something on the left, four or five inches above where the slug had actually entered.

We decided to give it a go, so she made a cut straight over where she thought she could feel the bullet. She burrowed down a couple of inches and there was the slug. She used the tweezers to pull it out. Then she cleaned everything out and stitched me up. Never got infected. I don't think I even missed the next meeting. I just drove the car instead of riding the bike.

* * *

SHADOW, SNODDY and I were spending a fair bit of time together during the week, so we had a lot of opportunity to yak on. Snoddy told us about his mate Leroy, who he'd known for years, and who he really wanted to get into the club. The problem, as Snoddy told it, was that Leroy used to hang round the Comos before I joined, and for some reason Foghorn and Snowy didn't like him and had given him the boot.

The way I saw it, though, there were blokes coming into the club that weren't half as good a quality of bloke as Leroy. I got to know him and he was big and strong, but more than that – Leroy had plenty of heart. Shadow and I met him a few times and on each occasion found him to be a top bloke.

Shadow, Snoddy and I agreed that at the next meeting we'd put it to the club that Leroy be made a prospect. If Jock, Snowy and Foghorn didn't like it, well, then we'd put it up again at the following meeting. We'd keep putting it up until they got sick of it or they ran out of excuses. And that's exactly what happened. I couldn't even tell you how many meetings it took to get Leroy into the club. But when we finally did there wasn't a happier bloke.

When he got his colours eleven months later he was picking blokes up everywhere and throwing them around. He had Lout straight up above his head, like a rag doll. After that he came around and thanked Snoddy, Shadow and me. We were shaking hands, and he was squeezing mine and I was squeezing his. We stood there for about five minutes just shaking hands. Neither of us was going to give up. Finally Shadow came over and said, 'I think youse have been shaking hands long enough.' I think Shadow could see that me and Leroy were a lot alike. In fact he was a lot like all us Campbells.

One night at the clubhouse I saw Chop carrying Leroy's colours around, and Bull carrying round Snake's colours. I thought, What's going on here? I fronted Jock and he told me that he'd heard there was another outlaw club over at the Sundowner pub at Bankstown and so he'd sent Leroy and Snake over to blend in and suss things out. Hence them leaving their colours behind. I said to Jock, 'You don't send fuckin' Leroy and Snake out anywhere together. You know what's gunna happen.' Because Leroy was like Snake – if someone gave him a dirty look it was on. Neither was the type of bloke you sent somewhere to be inconspicuous.

I headed straight out to the Sundowner.

The Sundowner was a pretty rough pub at the time so they'd hired some big blokes as bouncers. I rocked into the lounge where they had the bands on, and there were chairs going everywhere, bouncers lying on the floor. Here in the middle of it all were Leroy and Snake. Leroy had some bloody hunk of wood and Snake had a chain that he used to carry, and they were bashing the shit out of people left, right and centre. This big bouncer, six foot five with long hair, came running in and as he got near me I put my arm up and hit him in the throat. His head stopped but his body kept going, so he ended up bouncing on his back on the floor. I went over and grabbed Snake and Leroy: 'Get back to the car.'

As we were walking through the car park, Leroy noticed a car with a couple of cases of beer and bottles of scotch sitting on the back seat. He punched out the window, opened the door, picked up the two cases and gave Snake the bottles of scotch. They marched off to their car and I followed them back to the clubhouse.

IN JANUARY 1983, Roach got into a blue at the Lone Star Tavern, near Chinatown in Sydney, with two blokes from a club called the Loners. Snake, Gloves and Dukes jumped the Loners. Next thing they knew another Loner ran in with a sawn-off shotgun and pointed it at Snake.

'Call your mates off,' he ordered Snake.

'D'ya want me to come over there and shove that thing up your arse?' Snake replied.

Dukes intervened to calm things down and negotiated for the Loners to leave without further trouble. They backed out of there quick smart and took off with the coppers on their tails. Everyone made it home safely, but that night was the start of a war between the Comos and the Loners. The Comos didn't let any club put it on us, especially using firearms.

From then on, every time we saw the Loners, whether there was one of them or ten, we kicked the crap out of them. It wasn't long before they took off their colours and went into hiding.

We knew they had a clubhouse somewhere up in Kings Cross, so Sheepskin and his Strike Force were given the job of tracking the place down. It took them about two weeks. Then we had a special meeting where it was decided that Sheepskin, Shadow, Leroy, Davo and Lard, along with a few members of the Strike Force, would hit the Loners' clubhouse, which they did.

They wrecked the joint and everything in it, but the Loners had it fairly well fortified and had an escape route over the back fence and down laneways, so the members got away.

We'd made our point, though, so after that I came up with a plan to organise a peace meeting with their president and sergeant; we wanted to declare a truce. One of our members, Zorba, knew the Loners' sergeant, Julian, so he put the word out round the Cross that he wanted to meet up with him. Julian eventually fronted and he and Zorba arranged the meeting for midweek at the Milton Hotel at Auburn.

On the night of the meeting, Jock asked me and Snake to join him and Kraut on a run down Parramatta Road in Kraut's Commodore.

'Why?' I asked.

'I've got some information that the Loners are bringing out a lot of heavies from the Cross,' Jock said. 'All these Islanders and Maoris are gunna be waiting down the road from the Milton for a call to come and hit us.'

So we took off down the road, but when we reached Strathfield I said, 'There's no one down here. I don't think there's gunna be anyone hiding this far away. The Milton's eight K back.'

So Kraut chucked a U-ey and as we were heading back towards Auburn we spotted a bike coming towards us. As it passed we saw the rider had a set of Loners' colours. I got Kraut to do another U-ey and we followed him for two or three K before we pulled him over. He was all bloodied up and beaten.

'What happened to you?' I asked him.

'Mate, as soon as we pulled into the Milton all your blokes jumped us.'

'Nah,' I said. 'They all knew it was a peace meeting.'

I asked him where his president was and he said he didn't know.

'So what exactly happened?' I asked again.

'We pulled up at the hotel, me and the rest of me members, and before we were even off the bikes a whole bunch of your blokes attacked us with baseball bats and started stomping us. I was lucky to get away.'

I let him go and headed back to the Milton. All the way I was turning the bloke's story over in my head. It just didn't add up. But then it occurred to me that Jock had set me up; that the ride down Parramatta Road was just to keep me and Snake away from the hotel so that Jock's Strike Force could hit these blokes and finish them off.

By the time we arrived at the Milton there was no one there, only a whole lot of blood on the footpath. We headed back to the clubhouse, where my fears were confirmed. The Strike Force were strutting around like great victors. The rest of the blokes were real down in the mouth, because they knew it was supposed to have been a peace meeting.

The whole thing had been a ruse to lure the Loners out. Jock and his Strike Force were the only members who'd known about it. As soon as the Loners rocked up they grabbed the bats from the ute, knowing that once the fighting started the rest of the members would be obliged to join in. I guess Jock figured that I was the only one who might have stood up to the Strike Force and put a stop to it.

They'd taken a few sets of Loners colours, but most of the Loners had made it back to their bikes and got away.

At the next meeting I got up the Strike Force and had a go at Jock. 'You arranged for a peace meeting,' I said. 'It was a truce. There wasn't supposed to be any punching on or anything like that. How are other clubs ever gunna take our word now? How are they gunna believe they won't be attacked the same way the Loners were?'

I asked Zorba if he could arrange another meeting with the Loners.

'I doubt it,' he said, which I thought was fair enough.

'I don't wanna see the club as a whole,' I said. 'I just wanna meet the president and the sergeant. There'll be me and Shadow, no one else.'

Somehow Zorba managed to tee it up and we arranged a meeting at Maxim's Motorcycles in Leich-hardt. As promised there was me and my brother Shadow, and the Loners had their vice-president, Bernie, and their sergeant-at-arms, Julian. After the ambush at the first meeting, their president hadn't wanted to come. As it turned out their president, Kiwi, was actually the bloke I'd pulled over that night, riding his motorbike down Parramatta Road – the one who told me he didn't know where his president was.

So me and their vice-president had a talk and I explained to him what had happened, told him it wouldn't happen again. I gave him two options. That one, we'd close their club down, or two, they could come over as a prospect club for the Comancheros, called the Bandoleros.

'You got my word youse won't be touched,' I said. 'No matter what goes on. If you decide to break up and go your own way, you won't get hunted down or anything like that.'

'So what's the go with coming over as a prospect club?' he asked.

'You'll run yourselves,' I explained. 'You'll be a separate club. But as we see members of the Bandoleros progress, we'll grab 'em and pull 'em into the Comos. So you'll be like a feeder club, a patch-over. There might be some of youse stay Bandoleros for years, there might be some of you only stay a Bandolero for six weeks.'

Bernie said he'd take it back to his club. I gave him my phone number and he said he'd get back to me.

Two days later he phoned to say that some of the club had decided to leave and become independents, but that most had agreed to join up and become Bandoleros, with Bernie as president. I told him I'd deliver the good news to the club at the next meeting.

Unbeknown to me, though, in the meantime Jock had again gone behind the club's back and ordered his Strike Force to hit the house of the Loners' president, Kiwi.

I don't know exactly what went down, we heard all different stories. All we knew was that later that week the Strike Force rocked up at the clubhouse bragging about it; how Kiwi was cowering on the floor and all this sort of stuff. We heard from other people that the Strike Force had come in with baseball bats and guns, and smashed up the joint, thrown his missus round and threatened his kids.

I can only assume that to Jock's way of thinking, he figured that if he intimidated Kiwi he could get the Loners to become Bandoleros. If he'd just waited till the next meeting he'd have found out that I'd already got them to do that. And that Kiwi wasn't even a Loner any more. He was one of the members who, after our offer, had decided to drop his colours and ride as an independent.

Once news of the hit on Kiwi's house spread through the rest of the Loners, we lost a third of the blokes who'd promised to become Bandoleros. They didn't want to join a feeder club for the sort of blokes who would hit someone's home. It was a real bad look.

It was the lowest I'd seen Jock stoop and it caused a real stink in the club. Not only had he snuck behind the members' backs yet again to continue on his rampage, but he'd hit this bloke at his home. I went past Kiwi's place after the hit and there were kids' toys out on the verandah and the lawn. There is no more cowardly act than going to a bloke's house where he's got his missus and kids. It's a pet hate of mine. The thing that surprised me most was that, as sergeant of the Strike Force, Sheepskin had been involved in the whole thing. He just wasn't the sort of bloke to go to someone's house. He was like me: you stood toe to toe with a bloke and punched on. Why Sheepskin would've gone through with it, I don't know. All I know is that as much as we were mates, he was real tight with Jock too.

In any case we went ahead with setting up the Bandoleros. The ex-Loners came down to our clubhouse and Jock handed them their Bandolero colours. As usual Jock saw it in military terms: he'd say we could always use the Bandoleros as cannon fodder in the next war.

The Bandoleros got a clubhouse out at Concord Road, Concord and within a matter of months they had the whole place set up. They held a lot of dos, usually of a Friday night, which we'd go to, and then they'd come to our dos on Saturday nights. It was a good way of supporting each other's clubhouses, because a lot of money went over the bars.

Bernie became president of the Bandoleros and me and him started spending a fair bit of time together. We became good mates. He was a funny bloke, though. Other than the shoulder-length hair, if he didn't have his deck and leather jacket on, you wouldn't know he was a biker. He was a tennis coach and lived in a real posh house on the north shore. He played in club-grade tennis tournaments and had a straight wife.

NOW THAT we were over fifty strong, counting members and prospects – and with the Bandoleros to use as cannon fodder, as Jock put it – Jock was back in war mode. This time he wanted to wipe out a Christian club called the Brotherhood. The idea didn't go down too well with the club, because there was an understanding among outlaw bikers that Christian clubs were off-limits. But Jock was adamant that he was going to get rid of them.

'Whaddya wanna do that for?' someone asked.

'Their rockers are black and gold, same as ours,' Jock replied.

'They're not even an outlaw club,' I said. 'Why don't we just talk to their president and ask them if they'll change their colours?'

We agreed that was the way to go, so we arranged for the president of the Brotherhood to come over on a meeting night. When he turned up, I could see straight-away the Strike Force was ready to stomp him. I went out the front and told this bloke to piss off, but he refused.

'No,' he kept saying, 'I wanna talk to your president.'

'Piss off,' I repeated, 'or you're gunna get hurt.'

He stood his ground, so I backhanded him and sat him on his arse. It was a lot less than what the Strike Force would've done to him. He finally got the message and was just about to get on his bike when one of our fellas started laying into him. I pulled our bloke off and told the Brotherhood president to fuck off, which he finally did.

We went back into the meeting and got into yet another heated argument between the members and the Strike Force. It was becoming all too familiar. But the club had the numbers so this time we won the battle. We voted that we wouldn't be going to war with any Christian club.

AROUND THE same time, Leroy was arrested over a matter that I won't go into, but he was thrown into Long Bay on remand. I arranged a roster between the members and the prospects to make sure Leroy would have a visit on every visiting day, and we assured him we were doing our best to get him bailed out.

Me and Snoddy went to Jock and asked him for some money from the club account to pay Leroy's surety.

'No, no,' Jock said, 'that's me war fund.'

'War fund?' said Snoddy. 'That money's supposed to be there in case a member gets in the shit.'

'I can't help it if he got himself into it,' Jock said. 'He'll have to get himself out of it.'

Snoddy and I knew full well that money was there to help members so we kept pushing Jock, kept telling Leroy we were working on it. But Jock wouldn't budge.

So at the next meeting, me and Snoddy put it to the members that everyone put in a hundred bucks, or whatever it took, to raise Leroy's bail money. Everyone seemed all for it, but Jock's buddy Snowy was treasurer and he vetoed the idea. The plan went down the gurgler.

Snoddy pulled me aside after the meeting. 'Whaddya reckon's going on with the club's funds?'

'Whaddya mean?'

'We should have thousands in there but Jock reckons there's nothing.' The money in the account was raised through things like club dues and bar takings, which were not insignificant. 'He doesn't seem to have any trouble getting money for Vanessa's new car or that swimming pool he put in at the front of his house.'

'It's going to be hard to prove he's ripping the club off,' I said, 'seeing as Jock and Snowy are the ones that have got the books.'

SNODDY TURNED up at my place one night with Bernie. He'd brought him round to see my finger collection. By this time I had about thirty fingers in the jar, which I kept hidden in a false back in my bull terrier's doghouse.

No one would be able to get to them there, not if they wanted to remain intact. But I hadn't known Bernie long enough or well enough to show him that yet, so I said to Snoddy, 'Maybe in a few months' time, or when he's proved himself.'

'What have I gotta do to prove myself?' asked Bernie.

'I'll let you know when you've done it.'

Snoddy said that Bernie was hoping to find out a bit more about the clan.

'What, me brothers?'

'Yeah,' Bernie said. 'I've got to know Snake fairly well; he seems a real bad-tempered bastard.'

'He is,' I agreed.

'What about the others?' Bernie asked.

'Well Bull's a lot harder to set off but he's so big and strong he can do just as much damage,' I told him. 'If you like pig hunting, that's halfway to gettin' to know Bull. Shadow's a lot like meself: pretty quiet most of the time but when you provoke us we can be real nasty. Wack's another quiet one, but same thing, he could drop you with either hand.'

'What about Chop?' Bernie asked. 'He's not really your blood brother, is he?'

'Yes he is, and I wouldn't let Chop hear you saying otherwise. We picked him up when he got the boot from his own family and him and me and me brothers all did the blood brother bit. Then the day he turned eighteen he changed his name to Mark Campbell. So he's legally a Campbell and he has Campbell blood running through his veins. If you ever try and tell me he's not me brother you're in for a lot of grief.'

Bernie wisely changed the subject. 'So how'd Snoddy get a Campbell ring?'

'That's a lot harder to earn than your patch,' Snoddy said. 'And it was probably the proudest moment of me life when I was accepted into the Campbell family.'

'Yeah, there's only four other blokes who got 'em besides Snoddy, and that's Gloves, Dukes, Knuckles and Roach. And it took 'em a long time to earn 'em.'

'So what does your Mum reckon about you being in the club?' Bernie asked.

'When you've got the best mum in the world – no, make that the universe – what do you think?' I said. 'She supports us in anything we do. Just remember, she brought up fourteen kids mostly by herself. Me old man died pretty young.'

'I never had a real family until I joined the Camp-bells,' said Snoddy. 'Ever since I got this ring I go to Mum's birthdays, I go to the sisters' parties. I belong to two families, which makes me bloody lucky.' The other family Snoddy was referring to was the club.

Before he headed off, Bernie reminded us that the Bandoleros were throwing a party that Friday night and were going to have a pig on a spit and a stripper. I said I'd be there but it wouldn't be until late.

PARTY NIGHT came, and most of the Comos were there, along with all the Bandoleros. I was off working when I got a phone call from Bernie telling me to come over; there'd been some trouble.

When I rocked up, Jock had just arrived and was talking to his Strike Force. Bernie pulled me aside and told me that the Strike Force had turned up halfway through the party and Kraut had started throwing his weight around. He'd had a shot at Rua, one of the Bandoleros, then set his sights on Shadow. Bernie said Kraut followed Shadow around the clubhouse, egging him on and making smart remarks. Eventually Shadow approached Bernie and said, 'Look, I've had enough of this cunt. I'm not gunna make any trouble here at the clubhouse, I'm gunna take him down the park.'

'Fine, we'll come down and make sure everything's fair,' Bernie said.

So Shadow and Kraut went down to the park about four houses along from the clubhouse. It took about ten seconds for Shadow to flatten Kraut. He was out like yesterday's newspaper, as Bernie put it.

Having heard the full story I walked over to Jock, taking Bernie with me. I got Bernie to tell Jock what had happened. Jock wasn't satisfied with Bernie's explanation, but said we'd sort it out on meeting night.

Come meeting night, Kraut declared he wanted Shadow's colours for one member hitting another. Davo stepped up in Shadow's defence: 'If anyone's colours should be taken it should be yours, Kraut. You offered Shadow out in the first place and Shadow ignored you and tried to walk away. But ya kept following him. Anyone else in the club would have done the same thing.'

Shadow finally spoke up. 'I don't want his colours. As far as I'm concerned it all ended in the park.'

That was as far as it went, because next thing Snowy got up and surprised everyone: 'We've got more important business to discuss. We're going to war.'

The room erupted with everyone wanting to know what club it was.

'The Gypsy Jokers,' Snowy said.

'Whaddya wanna go to war with them for?' Davo asked.

'They've got the same colours as us,' Snowy said. 'Plus they're moving out of Fairfield and into Parramatta, which is our territory.'

Davo, who was usually pretty quiet in meetings, couldn't contain his disgust. 'You've gotta be kidding. They've been goin' as long as us and suddenly you decide you wanna go to war with 'em because of their colours? For fuck's sake, they're similar, but they're not the same; they've got a maroon strip round the border.'

'I don't care,' said Jock. 'We're gunna wipe them out.'

Davo wasn't going to leave it. We'd all reached our limit with Jock, and Davo wanted to take him on. He continued to challenge Jock, and judging by the look on his face he was about to punch the living shit out of him. I stepped between them to ensure Davo didn't flatten him. The two were about the same size, but Jock had his Coke-bottle spectacles and Davo was one of the better fighters in the club.

'Why all of a sudden d'ya wanna wipe them out now?' Davo continued. 'Is it just because our club's the biggest in Sydney?'

'Yeah,' Jock said. 'We'll prove we're the toughest club in Australia.'

I could feel my temperature rising, too. 'We don't have to prove it,' I stepped in. 'We know we are.'

'Yeah,' agreed Davo, 'whadda we gotta prove it for? There's not a single club who comes into the whole of

Parramatta any more. War and Peace is the only night-club in the whole area where you can get a drink at two am, but not one club will go there because they know the Comancheros will stomp 'em. We're already the toughest club in Australia.'

'Well I'm the president,' Jock argued, 'and you're only a member.'

'You're only president because members put you in the job,' I warned him. 'It'll only take one meeting to vote you out.'

It didn't worry me provoking Jock. I knew he wouldn't have a go at me, or Davo for that matter. In fact Jock would've been counting on the fact that I would step in and stop Davo from thumping him, because I was the one who'd brought in the rule that one Como couldn't fight another. But I was as pissed off with him and his war attitude as anyone. And all this in-fighting just wasn't how a club was supposed to run. Things had been building up long enough. I turned to Jock and let him have it: 'Look, if this is the way the club's gunna be run, like a fuckin' military outfit, and all you and the Strike Force wanna do is go round hitting club after club for no reason, I'll leave. I'll get me colours and you can have 'em.'

And with that I walked out of the meeting. Most of the club followed, then Jock and Kraut came out too. I think having seen all the blokes walk out with me, Jock must have realised he was on the verge of losing his club.

'Look, Caesar, ya can't leave,' Jock said.

'Come on, big fella,' Kraut joined in. 'Come back inside. Let's talk it over.'

'The only way I'm coming back into that clubhouse is if all this shit about hitting other clubs stops. I'm sick to death of the plastic gangster mentality that a few of this club have got. I'll be the first to go to war with a club if they hit our brothers. If something happens to one of our old ladies, I'll be standing right alongside you. But I'm not gunna hit a club for no good reason.'

'Well we're not going to now,' said Kraut, 'so let's go inside and talk about it.'

Mousey put his arm around me. 'Come on, Caesar. If you leave, I'm leaving, Davo's leaving, there'll be no club.'

So we went back inside and the meeting went on. Things were said that I can't repeat, but it was finally agreed that for the club to go to war it had to be a one hundred per cent vote.

The resolution lifted the members' spirits. I'd seen the blokes becoming restless over the last couple of years; they didn't like the drills, they didn't like some of the prospects that were being rushed through and patched up. But after things came to a head at that meeting, some of the tension eased off. Actually, the next month was pretty good. But it didn't last.

CHAPTER 9

It was 1983, and I was riding along behind Knuckles. Dukes was in the pack too, plus a couple of others. I don't know whether Knuckles just got into a daydream or something hit him in the face – because he didn't have sunnies on – but all of a sudden he swerved and ran straight into the pointy end of a cement lane divider. He went up in the air, the bike went up in the air, and then he came down again, crashing onto the road with the bike landing on top of him.

We pulled the bike off him and got him to Westmead Hospital, where he was operated on straightaway. They put a shunt in his forehead to relieve the pressure inside his fractured skull, his brain had swelled that much. It looked to me like a little garden tap was coming out of his forehead. His body was all banged up, too. It was a pretty bad crash. There were times there when the quacks thought we were going to lose him.

One of our members, Porky, hired a room in intensive care, which they had for friends and relatives, so he could be close to Knuckles in case anything happened. Porky spent the first week more or less living there. As Knuckles clung on, other members started using the room to give Porky a break. Every night there'd be at least fifteen or twenty Comos up in the waiting room outside. We knew that most of us couldn't get in to see him, but everyone felt that they had to be there anyway. The nurses got used to this big bunch of bikers hanging round. One nurse came up to me and said, 'You blokes have changed my opinion of bikies. I've spent most of my career in intensive care and I've never seen a bunch of blokes care so much about another man in my whole life.'

Gradually Knuckles came out of the woods, but he wasn't the same man. The accident left him with severe headaches, no sense of smell or taste. His memory was shot and he was often disoriented.

The whole club pitched in to get Knuckles back on his feet. He moved in with his brother Dukes while he was still recovering, and Dukes and I took turns to look after him; the accident had caused him to become violent with anyone other than me and Dukes. When he was right to move out on his own again, the club rented a house for him and his old lady, Wendy, filled it with furniture and put on the phone and electricity. Wendy had just had a baby boy, Harley, so her time was taken up with him and they had no money coming in. She would sneak the bills out the window to us – because Knuckles would never have asked for help – and the club would pay them. We looked after our own. Especially his brother Dukes, who couldn't have loved a brother any more than what he did.

While Knuckles was still in hospital, Jock gave another member, Opey, and me the task of finding a new clubhouse. We'd outgrown the one at Granville, and it was time for something a bit more flash.

Opey rocked up to my place one day and said he'd found a place at Birchgrove. 'D'ya wanna come down and have a look, see if you reckon it's a go?'

So I got on my bike and followed him down through inner-western Balmain, into Birchgrove and to the bottom of Louisa Road, which ran down a narrow peninsula jutting into Sydney Harbour. Opey had a key and took me through the place. Soon as I got inside and saw the harbour views, the size of the place, I was rapt. The backyard ran right down to the water and looked straight onto the Harbour Bridge.

'How much?' I asked Opey.

'Three hundred bucks,' he said, 'but we can get in and have a coupla weeks free if we sign the lease later in the month.'

'Take it.'

At the next meeting we told everyone that we'd found the new clubhouse, so members started going down to have a look. Then we started moving the bar and fridges into the place. We had a couple of tables and coin-operated Space Invader machines that we set out on the verandah, which was all encased in glass, so that you could play games or just sit there and look out over the water.

We were still at Granville, just moving things in

slowly, when Shadow and Chop rocked up to me before a meeting one night and announced that they were going to bring Jock up on a charge; they wanted his colours.

I couldn't believe my ears. Whatever they had on him, they obviously reckoned it was enough for immediate expulsion – even for the president.

'What happened?' I asked.

'He's been screwing another member's old lady.'

'How d'ya know?'

'We were over at Five Dock this morning and saw Jock's truck parked out the front of _____'s house,' Chop said. (I won't name the member out of respect for him and his family.) 'We pulled up and as we were walkin' up to the front door, I looked through the winda and there was Jock screwing _____'s old lady.' Chop grabbed Shadow and pulled him over to check it out.

'He was going to town on her,' Shadow said. Chop knocked and _____'s old lady came to the door with Jock standing right beside her. Shadow asked him what he was doing there and Jock said he'd just dropped in to see _____. Chop and Shadow just turned round and left.

'You've got no doubt?' I asked them.

'No,' Chop answered. 'No doubt whatsoever.'

'Well you know the rule,' I told them. 'If you're gunna bring someone up and you want their colours, you've gotta talk to 'em before the meeting and give 'em a chance to explain.'

'There's no way he can explain his way out of this.'

'Have you told _____?'

'Yeah.'

'What did he have to say?'

'He was shattered,' Chop said. 'He took off on his bike and we haven't seen him since.'

'Is he here?' Shadow asked.

'No, and the meeting's about to start,' I said. 'Jock's not here yet either so you're probably gunna have to wait till the next meeting to bring him up.'

The meeting started and Jock only turned up halfway through – too late for Shadow and Chop to talk to him.

After the meeting, I called Jock out the back. Shadow and Chop came out and fronted him about what they'd seen. Jock denied it, but Shadow and Chop called him a straight-out liar. I told them to wait there for a minute and went and got Sheepskin, took him out the back. I figured we needed another member there who couldn't be accused of bias.

'Shadow,' I said, 'tell Sheepskin what you seen.'

Shadow told Sheepskin, and Chop confirmed it. Sheepskin slumped. He turned to Jock: 'You're a stupid fuckin' old fool. You're gone. You've done yer colours.'

I actually felt sort of sorry for Jock at that moment because he had started the club and now, for the sake of a fuck, he knew that come next meeting, he'd be out.

DURING THE following week we finished the move from Granville to Birchgrove, so we were well ensconced in our plush new clubhouse by the time of the next meeting. And it was shaping up to be a doozy.

We had all agreed we wouldn't tell the other members about Jock screwing another member's old lady. The member concerned had asked us not to, so out of respect to him we kept it just between Shadow, Chop, Jock, Sheepskin and myself.

Come meeting night, we were all sitting there in anticipation. Chop wanted to make the first issue on the agenda the taking of Jock's colours, so when he wasn't there on time we delayed the meeting for twenty minutes. But in the end he never turned up. Nor did he show up at the next meeting.

Half an hour into the fourth meeting since Shadow and Chop had sprung him, Jock rocked up at Louisa Road with his Strike Force. He strutted in and called everybody together like he had a big announcement. He waited for silence before beginning. 'I'm splittin' the club in two.'

We all just looked at him.

'I've started a chapter out west,' he continued. 'It's to be called the west chapter and I'm going to be president. The people in here are called the city chapter and, Caesar, I want you to be president. Whoever wants to come with me can leave now, but there's one rule in the west chapter, and that is that I have the final vote on everything. Whoever doesn't like that can stay here with the city chapter.'

'Fuck off,' Snoddy replied. 'Get outta the clubhouse. Anyone who wants to go with Jock, go now.'

'Yeah,' said Davo, 'fuck off, go join his Strike Force.'

I really think Jock expected three-quarters of the club to get up and follow him; he thought he was that special. But just one member, Bear, and one prospect, Bob, got up and went over to join Jock and his Strike

Force. Jock looked shocked to see the rest of the thirty-odd blokes stay put.

Before they left, Lard, who was staying at Birchgrove, approached Jock. 'We've got a national run coming up in October. What's gunna happen there?'

'Our chapter's gunna be going to Molong,' said Jock.

'Well if the national run is to Molong then that's where we'll be, too,' said Lard. 'We're still one club.'

'Youse can do whatever you want,' Jock said.

Oh, shit.

CHAPTER 10

O nce Jock had left the meeting Snoddy turned to me. 'So you're president.'

'Nah, you can be president,' I said. 'You're the life member. I'm happy with being sergeant.' I liked the job. I liked being the one out the front of the pack. To me the president's more of a figurehead; the sergeant is the bloke who really runs the club. He looks after the security, he looks after all the blokes, and I've always found that when members have problems – whether it be with their old ladies, financial or anything else – they'll go to the sergeant first.

The rest of the talk among the members was, 'Why did he do it?'

Everyone had their own ideas, but Shadow and I pulled Snoddy aside for an officers' meeting. I thought Snoddy deserved to know the real reason for all this animosity from Jock. We'd already asked the member concerned beforehand if it was all right to tell Snoddy and he'd agreed. So we got Snoddy to give his word that everything we were about to tell him must never be repeated. Snoddy had a Campbell ring so I knew I could trust him.

I told him about Jock screwing ＿＿＿'s old lady. Chop joined in: 'Jock's obviously split the club so that me and Shadow can't bring him up on charges.'

'That's the reason for the two chapters,' Shadow said.

Jock had declared that each chapter would run its own race and have its own rules. That meant we couldn't turn round now and vote him out of our chapter; he wasn't in it any more.

Snoddy shook his head. 'That cunning old cunt done it so he wouldn't lose his colours.'

We never told anyone else the story of Jock rooting ＿＿＿'s old lady. Even in years to come when our club got torn to pieces and picked over by investigators, when people used to say the split was over drugs or over Snoddy wanting to take over the club or me wanting to take it over, we never let on the real reason out of respect for the member who Jock had done the dirty on.

ONCE THE dust settled and we were officially in residence in Birchgrove, the first thing I did was go and see the bloke in charge of our local police station up at Balmain. I asked him to bring up his station sergeant, because like in outlaw clubs, I'd found that it was the crown sergeants or the station sergeants who really ran the coppers in the area. I introduced myself and told them that we'd moved in, and what the go was: that if they didn't harass us in the Balmain area they wouldn't get any shit from us. There'd be no blues, no yahooing. 'If you respect us, we'll respect you.'

They seemed to think that was fair and we shook hands.

As it turned out we got on real well with the local coppers. We kept to our end of the deal: we'd ride out of Balmain in a pack but keep to the speed limit, only opening up the bikes once we were on Victoria Road and out of the Balmain area. The other thing was, they used to have a lot of assaults in Balmain, but as soon as we moved in they all stopped. Because if we went to a pub and there were a lot of yobbos there, we soon cleared them out. We ended up being unofficial bouncers for most of the pubs. So we were liked in Balmain. The suburb might be wall-to-wall yuppies now, but back then it still had a bit of a bohemian spirit. The cops even ended up coming down to the clubhouse of a Saturday night to buy a feed and have a beer. The old ladies would make them up a plate of sausages or chops and they'd pay their five bucks. It was the cheapest feed around. And funnily enough the licensing police never hassled us either.

JOCK'S WEST chapter had left Granville and rented a big house on a corner just up from the Rosehill pub. But they had virtually no members to go with it. Just about everybody bar the Strike Force had stayed with us.

So Jock was keen to get the Bandoleros on board. The Strike Force sergeant, Sheepskin, went and saw

Bernie and told him that Jock wanted him to come over to the west chapter.

'What chapter's Caesar in?' Bernie wanted to know. 'I'm not doing nothing till I talk to him.'

So Bernie rang me and I told him what had happened. He said he'd call a meeting of the Bandoleros that night and ring me straight after. When he called back he said he and all but three of the Bandoleros were coming over to the city chapter. So that was the end of the Bandoleros. Bernie and his crew were made prospects for us and the rest of them just went independent. I think they could smell trouble.

The next month, September, Jock was due to marry his old lady, Vanessa. There were big plans for his bucks' night, but not one member from the city chapter got invited. There was already friction anyway but that left a pretty bad taste in our mouths.

Jock and his mates went up the Cross on his bucks' night and one of his Strike Force, Sparra, got into an argument with some Samoan or Tongan women, calling one of them a slut. A bunch of big Islanders jumped them and the whole west chapter copped a real good hiding. Most of them ended up in hospital.

It was embarrassing enough for us that Comos had been smashed – it weakened the colours even more – but then we found out that, in typical style, Jock was reworking the story to tell everyone that it was our chapter that got beat up.

If it had really been my blokes, I'd have been evening up big time. But Jock had his own ideas about retaliation. He found out where these Islanders drank and had two of his members ride past and throw half a house brick through the pub window. Stuck to the brick was a note that read: *This could be a bomb*. And that was it. As far as Jock was concerned he'd retrieved his club's honour.

It certainly wasn't over as far as the head bloke of the Islanders was concerned. He grabbed one of the hookers up the Cross who he knew hung round with us and told her to get a message to the Comancheros: he wanted to fight the head of the Comos. So this sheila came out to Birchgrove and passed the message on. She said the head Islander was a real big bloke, six foot five and seventeen stone, with tribal tatts on his chest and arms, and down his legs to his knees.

Even though we were now two chapters, Jock still considered himself to be the head bloke – 'El Supremo' – so Snoddy rang Jock's place to forward the message on. Vanessa answered.

'Can you put Jock on?' Snoddy asked. He could hear Jock in the background whispering, 'Who is it?' and Vanessa going, 'It's Snoddy.' Jock went, 'Tell him I'm not here.'

So Snoddy told Vanessa instead: that this bloke wanted to fight the top Comanchero and it was to be in three days' time, at two pm, in the alley behind the Rock'n'Roll pub at Woolloomooloo.

Jock never rang back.

The deadline passed and the hooker rang us again to say this Islander was really hassling her because no one had come in to fight him. Snoddy told Davo to tell the girl we'd be in the lane behind the Rock'n'Roll at two o'clock the next afternoon.

Come next morning we were at the clubhouse still waiting for Jock to call. We waited till eleven o'clock, but heard nothing. Snoddy turned to me: 'Well, big fella, looks like another job for you. Or should I ask one of your brothers?'

'No I'll do it.' I reckoned that if you weren't going to defend your patch, you shouldn't be wearing it. Any one of my brothers or Davo or Kid could have done it, but being sergeant I figured it was my job.

This Islander had a reputation for having a bunch of blokes hiding round the corner, and if he was getting beaten, fifteen or twenty Islanders would come piling out. So I had a car with four blokes tooled up for my back-up. We got there at two pm and they moved off to the end of the lane in the Holden. We waited till three o'clock, four o'clock. It looked like he was a no-show, but all of a sudden I saw all these black legs come running around the corner of the lane, and I thought, Fuck, there's hundreds of 'em. I know I like the shot of adrenaline when there's a chance I might cop a hiding, but this was ridiculous.

Then I realised it was just a couple of Koori football teams out for a training run. Phew.

I waited another half-hour before giving up on him. I started my Wide Glide Harley and rode down to where Snoddy and Shadow were parked.

'Whaddya doing? Snoddy asked

'I've waited long enough for this cunt. It doesn't look like he really wants to have a blue. He was all piss and wind.'

'I thought you woulda left an hour and a half ago,' Snoddy said.

'It's not really your fight anyway, Ceese,' Shadow said. 'It's Jock's.'

'When any cunt puts it on our club, it's every member's job to back up his colours for the honour of the club,' I said.

Snoddy suggested we take a drive through the Cross. 'This bloke shouldn't be too hard to spot. He's supposed to be about five-foot wide.'

We cruised through the Cross about four times but couldn't spot anyone, so we parked and had a look in a few of the clubs and pubs. Still couldn't find anyone answering the description, but we made sure people knew we were up there and that no one fucked with the Comancheros.

JOCK HAD his wedding and none of us were invited. The following month, we had our national run up to Molong. Despite all the bad feeling, our chapter was still determined to go. We were all Comancheros, after all. Jock led his chapter over the Blue Mountains west of Sydney and out through Bathurst, where they were pulled over and hassled by the cops – like the cops always did with bikers that went through Bathurst.

Our chapter decided to bypass Bathurst and went out through Oberon and up some back roads to a little place called Georges Plain. There's a tiny little stone pub there with a bar about thirty feet long. The owners put on a really good spread for us. It was great. Then we rode on to Molong. We came into town, thirty-four bikes, riding two abreast. Jock saw us ride in and was spewing at the sight of this big pack coming down the road. He only had about a dozen blokes at that time.

As we rocked up we could see there was some sort of ceremony taking place. I got off my bike and walked up to Sheepskin. 'Whaddya doin?'

'Jock's making Roger a life member.'

'How can he make him a life member? He's only been in the club six years. You gotta be in the club for ten.'

'Well that's what Jock's doing.'

I went back and told Snoddy, who was a genuine life member. He went off the deep end at Jock. I could see that some of the Comos from the west chapter had gone and picked up guns so I went up to Snoddy and said, 'Let it go, mate.'

Then I turned to Sheepskin. 'If youse make Roger a life member, you know you're gunna fuck up everything in the club. If youse lot are gunna break the rules, the blokes in our chapter are gunna wanna break the rules.'

Everyone was getting toey. The blokes from our chapter started coming over and it looked like there was going to be an all-in. But I was still sticking by my rule that I'd never fight anyone who wore the same colours as me. So I had a word with Sheepskin and told him I thought it best that the two chapters didn't spend the weekend together. I calmed all our blokes down, got them on their bikes, and again rode out two-by-two, heading back to Georges Plain.

As always, I was last to start my bike. I saw Jock standing on the side of the road and if his face had got any redder his head would have erupted. If it had been anyone but Jock, I could have almost felt sorry for him. If he'd just kept the Comancheros as a bike club and run it as a bike club, he would have had the biggest club in

166

Australia. Probably the toughest club, too. Which was exactly what he dreamt of. But he stuffed it up with paramilitary fantasies – and with his dick.

When we got back to Georges Plain, everyone set up tents by the creek in a paddock alongside the pub and settled in for the night. Some of the brothers went swimming, the rest hit the pub and a night of partying began. Next to the pub was a pile of these big old round wooden wheels that Telecom carried their cables on. There must have been 200 of them there. We asked the publican if we could use them for firewood. He agreed and so we had huge bonfires raging all night.

Shadow had a six-man tent, and all the blokes that liked to bong on went in there and hit it hard. All you could see was smoke coming out of this tent. You'd get stoned just walking past. We were having a great time.

Later that night we were surprised to see the lights of two Harleys approaching. They rode straight up to us and it turned out to be two of the west chapter, Bear and Bob, with their old ladies. They were the only two, other than the Strike Force, who'd gone with Jock when he split the club.

Bear approached me and asked if he and Bob could come back to the city chapter. Bear's old lady, Sharon, came over too. 'Please, Caesar,' she begged. 'You don't know how boring it is over with Jock.' I called Snoddy over, told him what they wanted. He said all right, and with that, we partied on into the night. All the brothers and the old ladies had a great time.

Around five am I heard gunfire. Jock wasn't that stupid was he? I jumped out of my tent to find it was just Charlie trying to shoot a couple of ducks in the creek with his shotgun. He hit more water than duck. I took the gun off him and told him to go to bed or I'd throw him in the creek.

Later that morning we started packing up to head back to Sydney. Sharon came over and thanked me for letting Bear come back. 'Last night was just like old times,' she said. 'It was great.'

Snoddy came over. 'I wonder what Jock and his Strike Force are doing? How many hangers-on did you count there yesterday?'

'Not counting Bear and Bob, four,' I said.

'Well that makes twelve of 'em. And how many's over here partying? Thirty-six.'

Light rain started to fall as we got on the bikes and rode out in our Driza-Bone oilskins, our colours over the top. The colours must never be obscured. By the time we got up to Oberon it was real foggy. Snoddy and I were out front, keeping the pace down, riding two abreast. The blokes behind would hardly have been able to see us. As we rode through the mountains the rain just kept coming. You really had to love the idea of being a biker out riding with your club. And we did.

We made it back safely and everyone went to the clubhouse to thaw out. Which is better than Jock and his mob had done. We got a call to say they'd gone through Bathurst again, and again they'd been pulled over by the coppers. The cops defected four or five of their bikes, and then another bike caught on fire.

We were sitting around the clubhouse talking about what a weird run it had been when one of the blokes pulled out a little bandsaw and started getting stuck into the bar. The bar was made out of old railway sleepers that Davo had polished up. We'd brought it over from the last clubhouse where we'd all burnt our names into it with a soldering iron. Now as I watched I realised this member was using the bandsaw to cut out Jock's name.

Oh jeez, I thought, this isn't looking good.

ABOUT A week later, my brothers Bull, Snake and Wack, plus Snake's old lady, went to a west-chapter barbecue at the home of Tonka, who was in the Strike Force. As soon as my brothers walked in they got a bad vibe. Bull couldn't understand it so he asked Sheepskin what the go was. Sheepskin said, 'You and your brothers are always welcome as far as I'm concerned, but the rest of the chapter, especially Foghorn, don't want nothing to do with the city chapter.'

At our next meeting Snake and Bull told the club what had gone down and the attitude of the blokes out west. Coming on top of the bucks' night and the Molong run, it was pretty clear that something had to give.

In early November 1983, Snoddy, me and Shadow called a compulsory meeting. Everyone had to be there. No excuses. When everyone rocked up to the clubhouse, they could see Snoddy was in a sombre mood.

'What's wrong, Snoddy?' Davo asked.

'Yeah, what's wrong?' said Lard.

'I got told on Sunday that Foghorn has been going out to Bikers Limited and handing over sets of colours for those little brass badges,' Snoddy said. Bikers Limited was a bike club where a lot of bike enthusiasts used to hang out. You could join them by paying fifteen dollars for a little brass badge. Snoddy had heard that Foghorn was just saying to these blokes, 'You give us your brass badge and we'll give you a set of colours.' The west chapter had suddenly built up from less than a dozen members to thirty.

'Their chapter has become as big as ours in a matter of a month,' Snoddy continued. 'It's like you ride with the west chapter and if you can make it from one set of traffic lights to the next, you get a set of colours. I can't cop this. When I joined the club you had to do a minimum of nine months. Now it's more like two. I don't know how you lot feel, but I don't want to be a Comanchero any more.'

I got up and said that I agreed with Snoddy; there was no longer any honour in being a Comanchero. Jock was cheapening the colours by patching up every man and his dog, and the way the two chapters were going there was never going to be any brotherhood between us.

Snoddy replied, 'If I've got Caesar's backing that's all I need.'

No one spoke against breaking away, but there were questions thrown about, like: 'What are we gunna do if we're not Comancheros?' I got up and said, 'Well, we'll do what the majority of the club wants – burn the colours – and then we'll have a meeting and decide what we're gunna do from there.'

The meeting lasted till about four the next morning. Snoddy put it up for a vote and it was nearly a hundred per cent.

Snoddy was given the job of ringing Jock and telling him. We were all there at the clubhouse the next afternoon when he picked up the phone. It was a tough call to make but not as tough as some people have made out. There's been a myth put around that Jock was some sort of father figure to Snoddy; that Jock had found him wandering around as a homeless young bloke and took him in. That's even been talked about as the basis for a movie some people are trying to get up about the feud. But it was all just bullshit put out by Jock to make himself look more important.

Snoddy had been a merchant seaman before he met Jock. That's a pretty hard life. And he'd seen a lot of the world. He wasn't some lost kid when they met. They were mates, yes, but they drifted apart over the years. There'd been tension between them for quite some time.

I was listening in as the call went through. Snoddy aired some of our grievances: 'We're not gunna cop the west chapter giving colours away after five weeks, six weeks.'

Jock tried all his usual tactics but it was too late.

'We're closing down the city chapter,' Snoddy said. 'We're gunna burn our colours.'

Jock jacked up. 'No way. They're my colours. You bring 'em over here.'

'If you want the colours you come and get 'em,' Snoddy told him. 'And I'll get Caesar to give you a kicking while you're here.'

Jock agreed to us burning the colours.

He sent Sheepskin and JJ from the Strike Force to our clubhouse to watch the colours being incinerated. He wanted to make sure every single one of them went in. Sheepskin came in but JJ stayed up in the car with all the doors locked. A fat lot of use he'd have been to Sheepskin if we'd decided to give him a kicking. Not that we were going to, but a lot of blokes in the club didn't like Sheepskin because of the way he was always wanting to punch on with anyone who pissed him off.

Even with everything that had gone down between us, I, for one, still liked Sheepskin. He and I had a yak while everyone piled up their colours and got the fire going. I think Jock wanted Sheepskin to count them out but he turned to me and said, 'Are you gunna make sure they're all burnt?'

'Yeah.'

'Fuck it, that's good enough for me.'

We had all the black leather vests piled up near a forty-four-gallon drum that we used for fires on cold nights. A whole heap of different blokes picked up their colours and dumped them in. There was no ceremony about it. Nobody was counting. We just threw a few decks in, waited for the fire to recover, then threw in a few more. After the last set went in, we left the fire burning and everyone went inside. I walked Sheepskin out to the car and we shook hands.

Back in the pool room the only topic of conversation was: 'Whadda we do now?' Everybody seemed to have a different opinion.

'Well, look,' I said, 'let's have a bit of a breather and then in two nights' time we'll have a meeting and decide.'

EVERYONE TURNED up two nights later. It was a bit of a shambles at first. You had Snoddy and Shadow and others wanting to join the Angels, which I would've happily done because of Guitar and another good mate of mine there, Matchy. But there were other blokes in the club who hated the Angels. Some wanted to join the Rebels, but Kid Rotten said, 'If we join the Rebels I'm leaving.' Others wanted to go to the Nomads, and some to the Gypsy Jokers. I would've gone to any of them so long as the whole club had agreed; above all, I wanted to keep everybody together. But there was no club that somebody didn't hate. I could see it was going to be a long night.

We talked about just going independent but we knew that if we did that, all the blokes would drift apart because you need that set of colours to fight for and respect to hold you together.

Two hours in, we'd reached a stalemate. Me and Shadow went to the bar to get a drink and Shadow turned to me. 'What about we start a whole new club? We could reactivate the Gladiators.'

'Nah, I'm not gunna go through that again,' I said. And besides, there was another club up in Newcastle called the Gladiators and I didn't want to create any hassles with them.

'Well, what about the blokes Snoddy met in America? The Bandidos?'

'Yeah,' I said, 'now that might be a goer.'

We went back into the club room and called Snoddy over. Shadow said to him, 'Whaddya think about putting to the blokes that we start a chapter of the Bandidos out here?'

Snoddy was rapt. 'Fuck!' he said. 'I shoulda thought of that. They're like the old outlaw bike clubs.'

Straightaway Snoddy was up in front of everyone. 'Shadow's come up with a great idea. What about we all become Bandidos?' For the next half an hour everyone was talking about it, after which Snoddy called for a show of hands. 'All those in favour of becoming Bandidos.'

Every single hand went up.

Snoddy got straight on the phone to Ha Ha Chuck, president of the Albuquerque chapter in New Mexico. He explained what was happening and Ha Ha said he'd have to check with Ronnie Hodge, the national president of the Bandido Nation.

Five or six nights later, on a Sunday night, Shadow, Snoddy and me were waiting at the clubhouse for the call from Ha Ha. The phone rang and Snoddy picked it up. They spoke for a while then he held the phone away from his face. 'We've got the go.'

'You beauty,' Shadow said.

Snoddy turned to me. 'Well, whaddya think, big fella? Do we do it?'

'Well, we wanna keep all the blokes together. It's what we agreed on. Let's do it.'

'You got yourselves a chapter in Australia,' he told Ha Ha.

They spoke for a while about how it would work. Then Shadow and I spoke to our new brother and gave him our respects.

After we hung up, Shadow, Snoddy and I went to the bar. I got a lemon squash, Shadow poured an OJ and Snoddy fixed himself a spirit. We toasted our new club.

Next day we called up Junior and got him to come round. Snoddy had a photo he'd taken of a painting on

Ha Ha Chuck's wall. He said it was an exact replica of the colours: a Mexican bandit wearing a sombrero, with a sword in one hand and a raised revolver in the other.

He handed the photo to Junior, our resident artist. 'Can you draw up a set of colours from that photo?'

Junior scanned the picture. 'Yeah.'

'Then I want ya to take it to an embroidery place and get some colours made up.'

I think it took him about five days to get the first set of colours back from the embroiderer's. They only made the one set and Junior brought it round to me: 'Is this what ya want?'

'Yeah, that's it. That looks fantastic, Junior.' Junior went to grab the colours to take them back to the embroidery place.

'No, leave 'em there,' I said.

'But I need 'em to get the rest made up.'

'No you don't.' I knew from having colours made up in the past that they didn't need that set; they had them on a template. 'I'm keeping this set.'

I got the old lady to sew the colours onto a new vest that I'd had made up, and the first thing I did was ring Shadow to see if Snoddy was at his place.

'He's always here,' Shadow said.

'I'll be over in about half an hour. I've got a surprise.'

I rocked up to Shadow's place. Snoddy and Wack and a few others were there. When I turned round and showed them the colours they all wanted to know, 'Where's ours?'

'You'll have to wait a week or so.'

'Well then how did you get a set?'

'It's not what you know, but who you know.'

'Bloody Junior,' said Shadow.

I just smiled. Snoddy wasn't real happy because he wanted to be the first bloke in Australia to have the Bandit colours. Everyone in the club would've wanted to be first.

I took my vest off and put it on Shadow's table. They all picked it up and had a good look. It's normally not on to let anyone outside the club touch your colours. Like, you can't go into a pub and hang them over a chair. But we were all brothers in this together and they'd be Bandits soon enough, so I let them. After they'd all had a good look I put my vest back on. 'I'm off to the Cross to show off the colours.'

When I hit the Cross there were other clubs there as I'd guessed there would be. I sat there for about three hours, letting everyone have a good look at the first set of Bandido colours in Australia.

No one could ever know the feeling I had riding home that night knowing that a new club had just begun and I was wearing the first set of colours.

It was 22 November 1983. Because of the events of the following year, a lot of Bandidos to this day think the Australian chapter was formed in August 1983. But I'll never forget the real date. It was one of the highlights of my life.

For ten days I was the only Bandido in Australia. I was president, vice-president, sergeant-at-arms and member.

I went over to a place called S&S Cycles at Bexley,

which was owned by the Angels. I knew that Guitar worked there most days. I walked in and he could see I had a new vest on.

'All right, turn round,' he said. So I spun round. 'Oh no. Not the fuckin' Bandidos.'

'Yep.'

'Fuck. You're gunna make a lotta clubs unhappy.'

'Well that's their problem. Does it make a difference to us?'

'Nuh, I got no problem with the Bandidos. As far as I know, me brothers in America haven't got any problems with 'em either.'

We sat down and had a yak. I knew that once Guitar had seen them everyone in Sydney would know that the city chapter of the Comancheros were now Bandidos. We'd wiped our hands clean.

CHAPTER 11

I was offered the job of president of the Bandidos, but Snoddy told me he wanted the position. 'Okay,' I said, 'let's keep it the way it's been. You as president, Shadow as vice-president and I'll stay sergeant.'

The rest of the colours arrived back from the embroidery place and on the night of 2 December 1983 were handed out to the original members of the Bandidos Australia. First Snoddy and Shadow, then Roach, Bull, Tiny, Lout, Snake, Bongo Snake, Big Tony, Lard, Bushy, Bear, Wack, Chop, Porky, Davo, Kid Rotten, Gloves, Dukes, Knuckles, Charlie, Sparksy, Junior, Bernie, Lance, Zorba, Louie and Opey. There were twenty-nine of us, plus the five original prospects, Rua, Hooky, Sticks, Mouth and Bob. After everybody got their colours, we all went to the bar and toasted the club with an oath I'd made up: 'Cut one Bandido and we all bleed.'

There were thirteen club rules, but basically they could be summarised by saying you respected your brother and you respected your colours. So you didn't rip off your brother selling him a crap bike and you didn't try to crack on to your brother's old lady.

We swore to each other that the club would be run like a motorcycle club. We weren't going to have people rocking up in cars and then putting their colours on in the clubhouse like the Comos used to do. And we weren't going to be like a paramilitary organisation. We were there to ride bikes and have fun.

I used to be on my bike wearing my colours six or seven days a week. If I didn't have Donna with me, I'd be over seeing someone like Guitar or Matchy from the Angels, or Sy from Lone Wolf, or Metho Tom from the Nomads. It was like being in the Gladiators again. I could talk to blokes from other clubs without recrimination.

To celebrate this new freedom, we threw a big party. I invited Guitar and others from the Angels, and told Sy from Lone Wolf to bring along eight or nine of his blokes that he knew didn't drink too much or get wasted. I said the same to the Black Ulans. That way I knew there was a lot less chance of someone saying something wrong and starting a blue. The party went great.

I also paid another visit to the local coppers and asked to see the station sergeant. 'Look,' I said, 'you know we were Comancheros down at Louisa Road. Well we're Bandidos now. It's gunna be the same deal as when I first spoke to ya. You won't get any trouble in Balmain from us.' We shook hands again, and as I turned to leave I added, 'And youse are all still welcome to come down to our club on a Saturday night for a feed.'

At our first official meeting as Bandidos it was agreed that our inaugural run would be the Christmas run, and it would be to Port Macquarie. We'd leave the day after Boxing Day and stay through to the new year.

At the meeting we also decided we were going to kick off the club in a good way by doing something for the street kids in Balmain. There were a lot of them about then. Every member donated money and the old ladies went out and bought T-shirts, tracksuits, jogging shoes and toys. We invited all these young kids, most of them around eleven or twelve, who'd just been left to their own devices by their parents. Davo's dad – who we called Daddy Cool and was really close to the club – turned up as Santa on Davo's trike. They got off and all the kids mobbed them as they handed out the presents. The kids were ripping them open, just rapt. Then we took them all down to the front yard – which was really the backyard but we called it the front yard because it was down on the water. We'd set up tables and run an extension cord down for the fridges. The old ladies fed all the kids. There must have been a hundred of them all digging in and having a great old time. Then we cleaned up and all the members went back to have dinner with their own families.

We knew this club was on the right track.

THE DAY we left on the run to Port Macquarie was a rotten stinking day, pouring with rain and windy, but no one cared. We were out on the highway flying our new colours. We were all proud and riding high.

It took us a day longer than expected to get there, but it didn't matter. Once we reached Port Macquarie we set up in the caravan park and decided to make the local RSL club our base; they had bands on most nights through the holidays, and they had a couple of restaurants, including a nice-looking buffet. Me and Kid Rotten went in and I grabbed the head bouncer, who took me to see the president of the club. I told him what we were there for and that if he let us in we'd treat the place like it was our own, there'd be no trouble. If there was, I explained, I'd make sure that the member or prospect responsible was soon on his way back to the caravan park. And I made the same deal with the head bouncer that I had with Dave out at the Vicar of Wakefield – that if they got into any shit we'd back them up. It worked really well. His bouncers got into trouble one night and we stepped in and helped. Saved a few of them from going to hospital. The president of the RSL club later wrote us a letter thanking us for the way we'd behaved.

I also arranged to get a conference room with a big table for our meetings. So on New Year's Eve all the prospects were told to wait outside while the members gathered in the conference room to vote on whether we should patch up the new guys. Rua was the first prospect called in to be given his colours. As was the custom, he ended up being drowned in a sea of beer (and orange juice from me). Then we voted Hooky in and he came in and suffered the same fate. Then it was time to vote on Mouth.

I didn't trust Mouth and nor did Lance. There was just something about him. He seemed sneaky to me. But for some reason Snoddy wanted him in. I think it

Me at the beginning of the wild and violent years.

Sydney Gladiators in 1972. From the left: Snake, Bull and Wheels.

Me – President of the Sydney Gladiators in 1972.

Me during the Gladiator years in 1975.

I do smile sometimes. Not often. And not in this photo in 1985.

Me and my Scottish deerhound, Mingo, only nine months old here. That dog had massive balls.

Me and my bull terrier, Buck.

Me with Daniel and Lacey.

My brothers Wack and Snake. This is Wack's Fairlane.

Me and my old lady at a Bandidos wedding. I really do smile sometimes, usually when I'm standing over someone who's on the ground.

My old lady, Donna, in 1982.

A Bandido party in February 1984 at the Balmain clubhouse. That's Junior with his back to the camera.

This is Sheepskin in 1986.

Big Tony and Little J during the Port Macquarie run in January 1984.

Some of the original Bandidos. From left: Lout, Chop, Lard, Graham, Shadow and Tiny.

Snoddy and me at the Balmain clubhouse. This is the first anniversary celebration of the Australian Bandidos.

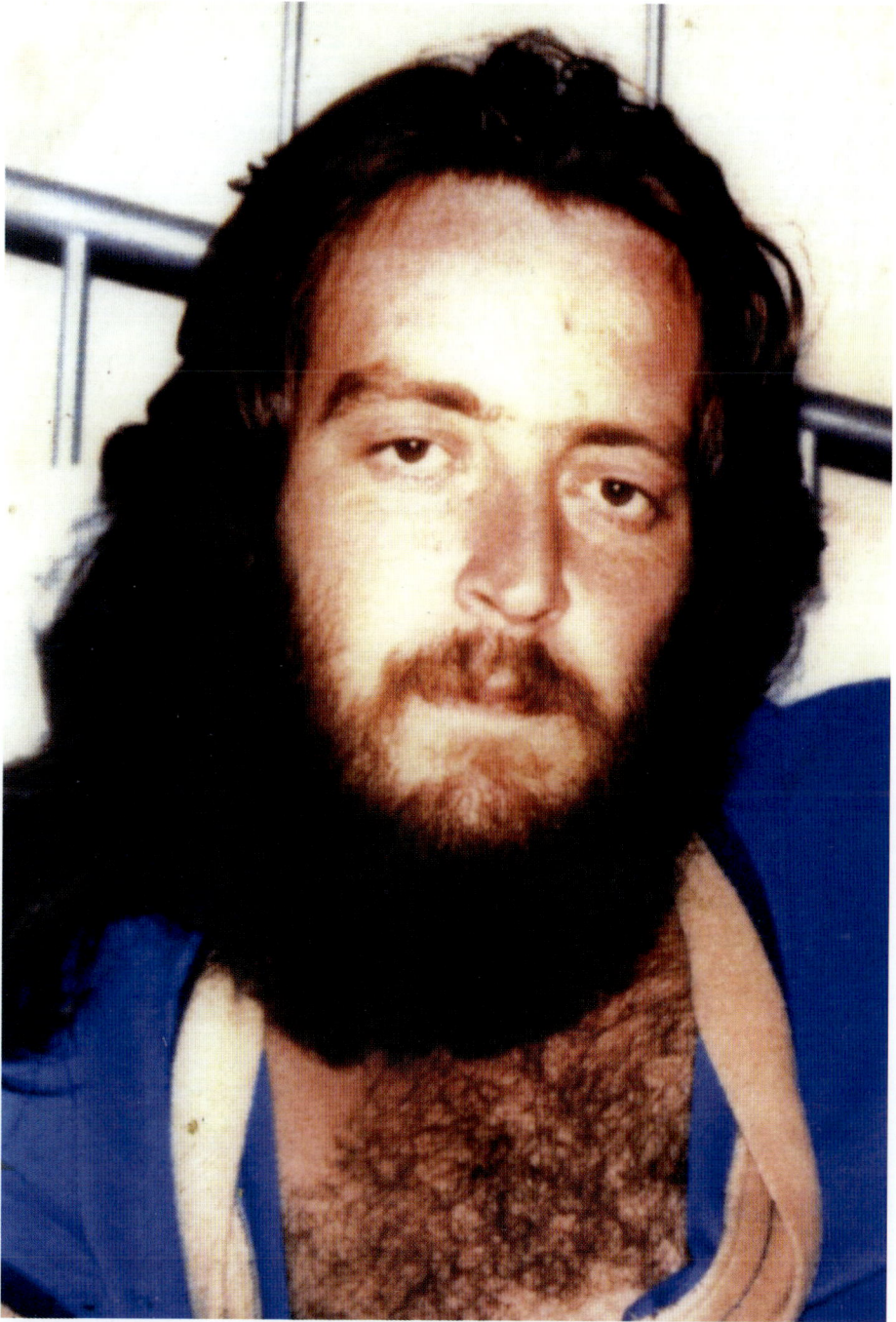

My brother Wack at Bankstown Hospital.

This is back when Donna was in kickboxing training in 1986.

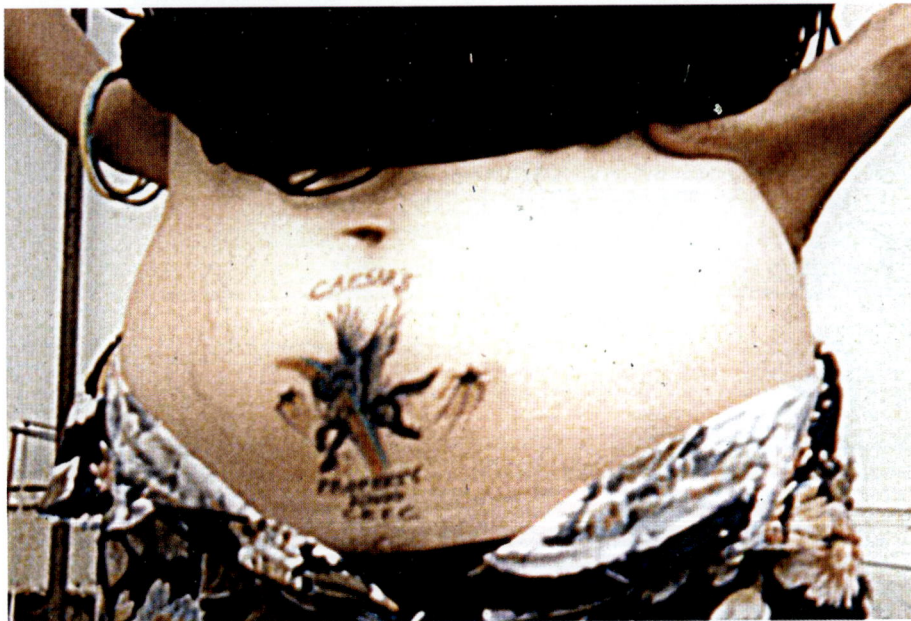

My old lady's first 'property of' tattoo. It reads: Caesar's property forever C.F.F.C. (Caesar's forever, forever Caesar's).

Explains itself! The world's number one club.

Donna's still riding. This time she has her little sister, Dee, on the bike with her.

'Mad' Max Murrell, my father-in-law, posing with his bike.

Me and the Blue Beast in June 2008.

Me on my '93 cubic inch Shovel Rigid. It has a '56 frame with a '76 motor.

Our two beautiful daughters. Chyanne (left) excels in kyokushin karate, and Lacey has a black belt in judo. Lacey has converted to Islam and now wears the hijab. She has three beautiful sons, Maalik, Yusuf and Ibrahim.

My son Caspar. He is an expert in six kinds of martial arts, including muay thai, kickboxing and Krav Maga, and has done a Navy Seals hand-to-hand combat course. Nearly as bad as me.

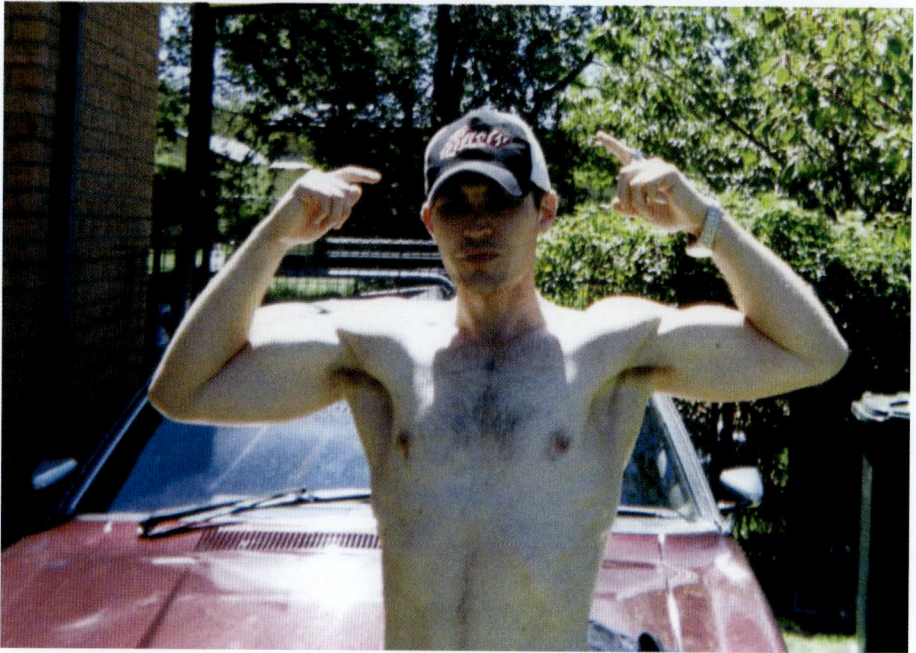

Our son Daniel. An amateur boxer, muay thai instructor and a black belt in judo. Carrying on the tradition.

This is the look you don't want to get.

came back to Snoddy having borrowed a fair amount of money off him. A prospect had to get one hundred per cent of the vote to get into the club so Snoddy had come to me earlier and asked me to vote for Mouth. I'd told Snoddy that I was never going to vote for the bloke. I thought it was even a waste of time keeping him in as a prospect.

Lance agreed, so Snoddy changed tack. 'Look, Caesar, we've been together so long, will ya just do me a favour?'

'What?'

'I know youse aren't gunna vote for him, but will youse abstain? That way you're not voting for him but youse aren't voting against him.'

Lance and I had a yak about it and Snoddy came back and pleaded with us some more. As a gesture of respect and love for Snoddy, we agreed to go along with it.

That's how Mouth got into the club. It was a decision I would live to regret.

The other downer for the week was when I found Knuckles wandering the caravan park close to tears because he couldn't find his caravan; his memory had never recovered after the accident. It was tragic to see such a fine athlete in that condition. Someone came up with the idea to write his caravan number on his arm and that seemed to help.

NOT LONG after our return from the run, journalist Richard Sleeman wrote a story in the *Sun* newspaper with the headline THE PRINCE IN CAESAR'S PALACE. It was about how we'd all helped Knuckles get back on his feet.

In it he wrote:

> when Phil McElwaine was hovering between life and death after a motorbike accident that fractured his skull, the sergeant-at-arms of his bike club thought hospital officials should be reminded of their patient's importance.
>
> 'I walked up to the doctors and told them they weren't dealing with just anybody,' Caesar, of the Bandidos bike gang, said yesterday. 'Phillip was the gold medal-winning boxing champion. I told them to make sure they looked after him.'
>
> When Caesar wants something done, it generally stays done . . .
>
> Caesar suggested I follow up the Phil McElwaine story and to make sure I wrote it well. It's difficult while your fingers tremble on the typewriter, but I'll try . . .

THE CLUB was on a high and everything was going great. The only one who didn't seem to be revelling in the good vibes was Snoddy. Soon after we got back from the Christmas run, he came over to my place looking down. He told me he didn't want to be president any more.

'Why?'

'Because I can't party.'

As president, he felt that he had to stay sober because he was responsible for everyone. But that just wasn't him. He loved hitting the pot and drinking like a fish. So he wasn't having a good time. Snoddy was a really good member and he wasn't a bad president. He had the respect of the blokes and he ran the meetings well. It was just that he didn't like getting offside with blokes he considered to be brothers; he didn't like telling them off if they needed telling off.

'Ceese, I want you to be president,' he said.

But I told him I didn't want the job. 'No, go back and give it another couple of weeks,' I said. 'If you're still unhappy we'll talk some more.' We agreed on that and a couple of weeks later things obviously hadn't got any better. He went and saw Shadow and said the same thing to him.

So at an officers' meeting one night at my place, we sat down and I said to Snoddy, 'Look, you go on being president. But if somebody needs pulling into line, I'll do it.' He usually gave that job to me anyway. 'You can still go out, party on, do whatever you want, be president, run the meetings, but me and Shadow will look after the club.'

'I can't expect youse two to be there twenty-four hours a day,' he said.

But Shadow and I had already worked out a plan where I'd rock up on club nights at five-thirty and stay till about one in the morning. Shadow would rock up to the club about ten pm and stay till nine or ten am on the Sunday. Shadow didn't drink either. He liked the bong but when he was doing his job as vice-president he was sober as a judge. With our plan, there was always going to be a clear-headed officer there to look after the members. To me, that was the job of an officer. And I would've taken a bullet for any member. That's how much I thought of them.

So that's how it went from then. We all adapted easily into our new roles. I got to know Snoddy pretty well during this time, but I still never asked him about his background. There were stories about his mother's death and things that happened to him as a kid. People used to hear these stories and ask him about it. He hated that. Suddenly they weren't friends any more. I could see it upset him so I never asked.

I was the same as him in that regard. I didn't like people pushing me for things. Some people had found out about the underground fighting and all I'd get was: 'Who did you fight? How much did you make?' I just kept my mouth shut.

The new order was great for Snoddy. It was like the old Snoddy came back. He was much more settled and full of life and that was good for the club. He loved playing his guitar and going to see bands. His favourite was a blues band called Ivory Coast.

He had good ideas for the club too. One of them was that he, Shadow and I should buy the Louisa Road house. It had been put on the market for about $350,000. This was an absolute waterfront with a view of the Harbour Bridge. We figured it would be worth a fortune in a few years (and it was).

It was a top old three-storey house built in the 1890s. The second storey was all glass at the front and we had the tables and chairs in there for the old ladies to sit in. There was a big pool room. We'd smashed out a wall and made a huge disco room with a bar. The bedrooms were upstairs, and downstairs you could go out onto the front lawn on the harbour where there was a grotto – a little cave in the rock face. We'd run some power leads onto the lawn and put the bands in there.

We'd have fridges and tables full of food. We had spits and hangis. There was a great view of the city lights at night. Harbour cruises used to come up and announce to the passengers that they were passing the notorious Bandidos clubhouse.

And there were always girls. Rua and Big Tony found that if they went over to Circular Quay around lunchtime they could pick up heaps of sheilas. It was only a couple of minutes on the ferry back to the Long Nose Point wharf right below our clubhouse. I'd rock up through the week and see these sheilas sunbaking on the lawn with Tony and Rua running round like kids in a lolly shop. Then the other blokes found out about the supply of girls and rocked up too. Everyone had a key to the clubhouse, so anyone could go in and take a sheila there. But they'd also go just to hang out. You could always get a feed. You could take a meal out of the freezer and cook it up on the big stove which had these great iron skillets. You'd put your money in a tin on top of the fridge, grab a drink from the bar, and go out and sit at one of the tables and watch the boats and the Harbour Bridge.

I'd walk in and grab an orange juice from the big dispensers like you'd see at a pub. And whenever I entered somebody would put 'Bad to the Bone' by George Thorogood on the jukebox, or maybe 'Wild Thing' by the Troggs. They were my songs and I'd always listen to them if I was pumping myself up for a fight.

As far as alcohol went, we had a deal going with the local bottle-o so we were selling beer for five cents more than what he paid for it. It was the cheapest beer in Sydney for members and their old ladies, although the outsiders who came over on a Friday night had to pay more.

On Saturday nights, club nights, all the old ladies were there, but on Friday night – boys' night – all the strays would rock up. There'd be women everywhere. One night there was a sheila up there who wanted to take on a fair number of the blokes while she had her monthlies. She took them up to the room that Big Tony rented from the club. When Tony got back to his room there was blood on the walls and all over his sheets.

I wasn't into any of that. Donna was all the woman I needed. In February 1984, she gave birth to our second child, Lacey. Daniel was three and a half by then and I'd spend most of my time at home with Donna and the kids. I wasn't the type to change nappies or wash them – that's women's work – but sometimes I'd feed them a bottle. I saw my role more as teaching them the other stuff about life, like what my dad taught me. How to handle yourself.

My routine involved going to the club every day to make sure everything was all right. I'd usually rock up to find Rua and Chop mulling up at the bar with the bong sitting there. I preferred them bonging on rather than hitting the spirits. I used to hate it if they'd been drinking spirits before we went to a pub because I knew there were going to be blues. Spirits made all the blokes nasty. Some more than others. And I had about eight in the club who got real nasty on spirits – my brother Snake being one of them. Lard and Sparksy too.

One night we were over at the Bayview Tavern in Gladesville watching a band, and Sparksy wanted a particular song played. The bloke said, 'I've already played it. I'll play it again in an hour or two.' Next thing I knew, Sparksy was up on stage and had the microphone cord wrapped around the lead singer's neck, strangling the bloke.

Not again.

So I got up on stage, dragged Sparksy off. 'That's it, you're back to the clubhouse.'

I grabbed two prospects and told them: 'Now you take him back to the clubhouse and you stay there with him.'

'But he's a member. We can't tell him what to do.'

'I'm your sergeant. You do what I tell ya.'

So they escorted him back to the clubhouse. When I eventually got back there, Sparksy came up all apologetic about carrying on at the pub. I said, 'Sparksy, mate, you're just gunna have to calm down. Drink beer or something.'

So whenever I saw those guys on the bong before we went out, I thought, Beauty. Haven't gotta watch them tonight.

But there was always something to watch out for. One night around this time we got into a fight with a huge group of Islanders at the Croydon Hotel. We kicked the shit out of them but afterwards I couldn't find Chop and Wack. I went outside and there they were, holding this Islander by the ankles over a brick wall. Below them, down in the cutting on the other side of the wall, was the railway station.

'What are youse doin'?' I wanted to know.

'Waitin' for a train,' they said.

'Will ya pull 'im up?' I said, like I was rousing on two naughty kids.

They pulled him up and thumped him.

I got all the blokes together and had a word with the manager. I said, 'Work out what your damages are and we'll pay half.' I got the blokes outside and as usual mine was the last bike to start. I was just about to give the signal to leave when half a house brick hurtled past Donna's head.

That's something you don't do: go near my woman. So I was off the bike and back into the pub punching on again. Everyone was off their bikes right behind me. All the blokes that were lying on the floor were getting stomped. Then we heard sirens so we all went back to the bikes.

Coincidentally, Big Tony was sitting in a holding cell at the Campsie police station at this point. He'd been off elsewhere and got picked up on a warrant. He heard the police radio going off. 'All police to the Croydon Hotel! All police to the Croydon Hotel! Bandidos rioting!'

He said he was in there cracking up at all the coppers running around looking for batons and shields. He said to one bloke as he was running out the door, 'You're gunna get ya head kicked in tonight.'

We'd all got back to our bikes and were riding down Croydon Road when suddenly there was just cop car after cop car streaming down. There were thirty-four of us there, I think, and I was out in front. Snoddy pulled up alongside me: 'Whadda we doin'?'

'We're goin' back to the clubhouse,' I said over the rumble. 'If it's gunna be a punch-on, it's gunna be back where we can put the ol' ladies and that.' So we gunned it. Thirty-four bikes that weren't going to stop for anything. Through red lights. Cars were parting. The sheilas were terrified. It was the most mighty roar of engines. We thundered back the ten kilometres to the clubhouse, put all the bikes away, sent the old ladies inside and lined ourselves up in the cul-de-sac, me standing out the front, waiting for the coppers.

They pulled up and a big D got out of the car second from the front. He looked a real smartarse and I thought, Ah, there's gunna be trouble tonight. But then a crown sergeant got out who I recognised from Five Dock.

I turned to the blokes. 'Just cool it and let me talk to this bloke.'

I walked up and told him how we were at the Croydon, that there were three young blokes there about eighteen years old, and they had a girl with them who was about seventeen. All these Islanders had tried raping the young sheila and we'd stepped in to save her. That's when the brawl broke out, I said.

The sergeant looked at me. 'And that's what happened, is it?'

'Oh shit yeah. She'd have been raped, prob'ly killed, if it wasn't for us.'

'So, all this trouble was because you were defending a young girl?'

'That's right. The boyfriend prob'ly would've been stomped to death too. Actually, you should be giving us an award.'

The detective butted in. 'I reckon that's a lot of bullshit.'

No shit, Sherlock.

Next minute, there was another siren and lights, and this paddy wagon was coming down the footpath towards us. The local sergeant and one of his blokes got out. 'I've heard over the radio what's going on. I'm just here to say that these blokes have never caused any problems in the Balmain area. I'd like to speak up for them.'

'You'd actually stand up for these guys?' the detective asked.

'Yes, sir.'

'All right.'

The big sergeant from Five Dock turned to me. 'Can I have a word with you?'

'Yeah.'

'Caesar, that was the biggest pack of bullshit I've ever heard in me life.'

'Well, now, did you want to get into a fight tonight?'

'No.'

'Well neither did I.'

I'd given them an out and they'd taken it.

Getting all the cop cars out of Louisa Road was another story. It was such a narrow street, lined with all the BMWs and Mercedes of the doctors and lawyers and famous writers who lived there, they practically had a demolition derby trying to leave.

ONE OF the proudest times I had with the Bandidos was once when I was on my own down at a pub in Balmain and there were about forty wharfies there, all making fun of the big bad biker thing. I was standing there solo, surrounded by all these wharfies, thinking, Fuck, I'm gunna be in hospital for six months. Luckily the barmaid knew me. Most of the pubs in Balmain had our clubhouse phone number. She rang the clubhouse and next thing I knew I looked over my shoulder and there was Kid Rotten, Opey, Charlie, Davo, plus Snake and my other brothers. All standing there. It's hard to explain, but I got this real warm feeling. Here was this bunch of blokes who'd rush down even though they knew they were going to be outnumbered. They were standing behind me, all ready to go, and telling these blokes, 'You want to take on one Bandido, you take on all Bandidos.'

They were living out the motto I'd made up for the club: cut one Bandido and we all bleed. It made me so proud to be part of this club.

THERE WERE four blokes hanging around the club – Tramp, Sleazy, Maverick and Scotty – and in about April or May 1984 we decided to make them prospects. Maverick was the brother of the chick Snoddy was going out with.

A couple of weeks after they'd been made prospects, Donna and I pulled up at the clubhouse on the Saturday night and Shadow had a real stern look on his face. I could tell he was agitated. He pulled me aside and said the new prospect Scotty had been fucking around with another club, causing trouble.

'What club?' I asked.

'The Lone Wolf.'

'Have you spoken to anyone?'

'Yeah, I've spoken to a couple of their top blokes.'

'What's their version?'

'Completely different to Scotty's.'

'Well get in touch with the blokes you were talking to and take Scotty out there. Just watch how Scotty reacts when he has to front them.'

So Shadow did that and reported back that Scotty had made a complete dick of himself and fucked up something bad. Shadow made an agreement with the Wolves that we'd take care of Scotty ourselves.

A lot of the blokes wanted to stomp the shit out of Scotty. But me and Shadow figured if that happened, he'd probably end up dead, so we came up with another idea. Seeing as he was a fuck-up, we thought we'd brand him with the letter F.

We brought in all the prospects so they could see what happened when you fucked up. I heated up an iron bar till it was red hot. Then I pushed it hard into Scotty's wrist to make the long straight part of the F. I smelt burning hair and flesh, and I pressed harder still. All of a sudden there was nothing pushing back against the iron. I looked to see what had happened and I was more than a little surprised to see that the metal was that hot it had just burnt through and out the other side of his wrist. I could smell the blood burning and hear it sizzling on the iron.

Scotty had not made a sound. But he looked very pale, like he was going to pass out. He had to sit down. Charlie stuck his head out the window ready to chuck. The rest of the prospects looked like they wanted to run.

Shadow told Scotty to get back up, that it wasn't finished. I'd pulled the bar out of his wrist and Shadow picked up a hot knife now and made the other two lines, completing an F that didn't look too messy, considering. Snoddy reckoned it was the most sickening thing he'd ever seen.

We sent Scotty to the hospital with the other prospects and never saw him again. Scotty had lied to the club and he nearly caused a lot of shit between us and a club that we were pretty friendly with. We didn't want to go to war with anybody. We'd left all that bullshit behind us with Jock.

UNFORTUNATELY, JOCK hadn't left us behind. He'd got it into his head that his honour had been impugned when we walked out on the Comancheros, and he was getting ready to avenge it. While we'd been having a good time partying and going on runs like a bike club should, the Comos had been busy recruiting.

I got a call from Leroy, who Snoddy and I had tried so hard to get out of jail. He was out at last, he said. And Jock had paid the bail.

We arranged to meet at the Royal Oak in North Parramatta and a big group of us went along to see him. As soon as we walked in, Leroy told us, 'You know if I had me choice, I'd be with youse.'

'Well why aren't ya?' I asked.

Leroy said that Jock had offered to bail him out, but only on the condition that Leroy give him his word that he'd stay loyal to him and do whatever Jock asked. Leroy didn't know at that stage what had gone down with the club; visiting him in jail no one had wanted to bring him down with talk of the split. So Leroy had given Jock his word.

Sitting there at the pub, we told him we understood his predicament.

'You all know what I think of you and that I love youse,' he said. 'You and Snoddy and Shadow were the ones that got me into the club in the first place. If I'd have known what was happening, I'd have told Jock to stick his bail up his arse. I'd have stuck it out in jail.'

'Sorry, mate,' said Snoddy. 'We were trying to get the money together to bail you out.'

'Well, it's done now and I've given me word.'

He more or less said he was sorry that he was going up against us. 'I'm not dumb,' he said. 'I know what Jock's got me out for.'

It was obvious to us too. Leroy was a big, impressive-looking bloke and he was about the only one Jock had who might stand a chance against my brothers or myself. It was a classic Jock manoeuvre.

We put talk of Jock behind us and had a drink. Leroy asked me how Donna was.

'Still the best-looking chick in the club,' I said.

'You're not wrong,' Leroy said.

'You been hitting the iron while you been in the Bay?' Chop asked. 'You're nearly as big as Ceese.'

'How big are you round the chest?' Leroy asked me.

'Fifty-three inches, unexpanded.'

'What about your arms?'

'Right arm nineteen and a half inches, left arm nineteen inches.'

'You're still a bit bigger than me,' he said.

'And they'll have to stretch you another four inches so we can be eye to eye,' I said.

We all had a good laugh. Shadow walked back from the bar. 'Sounds like you blokes are having a good time.'

'You still got the fastest bike in the club, Shadow?' Leroy asked.

'Caesar and Lout think they have, but Lout spends more time pushing that Pan than riding it.'

It was a good night. We chewed the fat and had a laugh. At the end, we all shook hands and Leroy said, 'I wish you guys all the best with your new club.' But there was something in his voice. He said it like he was apologising for something that hadn't happened yet.

CHAPTER 12

In June 1984, our member Junior went to a swap meet at the Rebels' clubhouse with his old lady, Cathy. As it turned out, Jock's two sidekicks, Foghorn and Snowy, were there with a Como prospect called Pee Wee who, as you'd expect with a name like that, was a pretty big unit.

They started following Junior around and insulting Cathy. Junior was only twenty-two and as strong as an ox, but everyone knew he couldn't fight to save himself. But everyone also knew that Junior had a bit of ticker and would never run away from a fight no matter how many blokes were lined up against him. The Comos knew that made Junior an easy mark. They kept pushing him and pushing him till he stood his ground and offered them on. It was just about to blow up when a Rebel came down and told them to take their problems elsewhere. So Junior left and, being the man he is, waited for Snowy, Foghorn and this Pee Wee prick down the road.

The Comos stopped and Junior asked them why they were insulting his old lady, he hadn't done anything to them. With that, Foghorn took a piece of a Harley fork leg he'd just bought and smacked Junior in the face with it, breaking Junior's jaw. Then Snowy and Pee Wee held him down while Foghorn stabbed him in the face, before they all started putting the boot in.

Junior was a mess. Cathy helped him back to the bike and they got up to Canterbury Hospital. I got a call from Cathy to say that he was going in for surgery and I raced up there as fast as I could.

The quacks said it would be a couple of days before Junior was able to talk, so I just went up there every day and sat by him until he came out of it. When he eventually could talk, his jaw was wired so he was hard to understand, but he told me enough. And it didn't surprise me. It was always Foghorn's go to be a tough man when the odds were in his favour.

'Whaddya wanna do about this?' I asked. 'Do you want the club to take care of it? Or do you want me to do it?'

'What would you do if this had happened to you?' he asked.

'Well, if it was to do with the club and the club had been insulted, I'd let the club know. But if me old lady had been insulted, I'd take care of it meself. Whether I got 'em one at a time or two on one or whether I'd use the baseball bat or an iron bar, I dunno, but I'd get the blokes meself.'

'You wouldn't involve the club?'

'No, I might get one of me brothers to help me if I thought I couldn't handle it, but I think I'd take care of it meself.'

'Well that's what I want to do then. It's personal. I'll fix it up myself.'

'All right,' I said. 'The rest of the club are firing up so I'd better get over to the clubhouse.'

When I got back to Louisa Road, every member was there, ready to rip heads off. I briefed Snoddy on what Junior told me. Then he pulled all the blokes together in the pool room and told them that Junior was going to handle it himself; that it was a personal issue, not a club issue. A lot of the blokes still wanted to go out and bash Comos.

'I know how youse feel,' I said. 'I feel like going out and punching those cunts' heads in meself, but we've got to respect the man's wishes or he's going to think that we don't respect him.'

Everyone agreed with this. A lot of the fellas headed over to the hospital to visit Junior. It wasn't a good night at the clubhouse.

The next day, the Comancheros' Strike Force sergeant-at-arms, Sheepskin, called me and, given what had happened to Junior, it wasn't a real friendly call at the start. Even though I personally liked Sheepskin I wasn't in the mood for exchanging pleasantries. But Sheepskin soon explained that he was ringing to see how Junior was and to ask me for Junior's side of the story. So I told him.

'I thought it would be something like that,' Sheepskin said. 'I heard Snowy and Foghorn's version and, knowing Junior, I figured that what they said was a bunch of shit.'

'What did Foghorn and Snowy reckon happened?' I asked.

Sheepskin said they'd claimed that Junior was running down the Comancheros and making fun of Jock, and he'd put it on them. 'That's why I was suspicious,' he said. 'I knew Junior wouldn't start any fight.'

He asked me to give him a couple of days and he'd get back to me. 'You've got me word that I'll try and find out what's going on.' He paused, then asked me, 'Ya know, is this gunna be an all-out blue and everything?'

'You'll find out one way or another.'

He rang back two days later and told me that he'd grabbed the nom, Pee Wee, and taken him out behind the clubhouse. Sheepskin told him, 'Now don't fuckin' lie to me or I'll smack your head in.' After about fifteen minutes Pee Wee told him his version, which was nearly identical to Junior's.

'Youse are lucky this time,' I told Sheepskin. 'Junior wants to front those three cocksuckers himself. It's not gunna be an all-in. But you can tell Foghorn and Snowy and that other prick of a prospect of yours that the next time I see them they're gunna feel me boot in their faces. And if it happens again I won't be holding me brothers back.'

'I sorta figured that was going to be your response, but there's not much I can do about it. Foghorn's in Jock's ear non-stop. This is heading for trouble.'

'I don't know why you won't just leave the prick. You know I've always trusted ya. You've always kept yer word. But being in charge of the Strike Force seems to be changing ya, Sheepskin. You're not the same man ya were when I first came round the club.'

I told him it was up to him to keep it cool on his side and I'd try to do the same with my brothers.

'Well I can only try me best,' he said.

'Well your best better be pretty good.'

NOT LONG after Junior's bashing, a few of the blokes decided to ride up to the Bull & Bush Hotel, thirty kilometres away in Baulkham Hills, after a club meeting one night. About eight or nine of them rocked up to the pub only to discover about ten Comos – or Condoms as we'd started calling them, because you had to be a dick to be one – already there. In the crowd, Big Tony recognised the prospect Pee Wee, who at about six three was easy to spot across the room. Even though we'd agreed we were going to let Junior square up himself, I suppose Big Tony just couldn't resist. He went over and picked up Pee Wee and threw him straight through a plate-glass window.

Snoddy was there too and he started laying in along with Bushy and my brother Shadow. Snoddy tried scalping some bloke and got hold of a little peanut they called Nugget. A Como called Dog also copped a beating. Our guys were outnumbered but the Comos just faded away.

Snoddy rang me later that night to tell me what had happened.

'Whaddya think'll come of this?' he asked me.

'We'll just have to sit back and see.'

IT DIDN'T take long to find out. Chop, Louie and Charlie were at the clubhouse one night in July 1984, pulling cones in the second-floor kitchen which faced down onto Louisa Road. Next thing they knew, bullets were flying through the wall, which was only made out of a thin ply. They raced to the window and saw that it was Foghorn and Sparra. The only damage done was to a small room at the back of the house which was made out of fibro. Some shotgun pellets had gone through the walls and a high-powered rifle bullet had hit some brickwork.

The neighbours called the cops, but when they turned up, Chop told them he didn't know what they were talking about. Outlaw clubs just don't go to the coppers because you know they're not going to do anything except try and lock someone up. The coppers like to think of themselves as the biggest club in the country, and when they run into a bunch of blokes who won't abide by their laws they don't like it.

About two nights later, there was a second shooting at Louisa Road. There was no more damage, but the neighbours called the cops again.

We'd always known Jock wouldn't fight us head on; too many of us could fight. Our front line was like bull-dozers and the others were a pretty handy back-up. You didn't find blokes like that at bike shops.

It was clear Jock would just continue taking sneaky pot shots at us.

WE USED to go to the Royal Oak at North Parramatta fairly often – even though it was in Como territory – because one of our members, Lout, was the manager there. One night Lout was alone at work when all of a sudden Jock, Leroy and another Como walked into the bar. Jock was carrying on about how there weren't going to be any Bandidos in Parramatta. He was making a big statement out of it: here they were, three Comos unafraid to stroll into a Bandit pub.

That was the extent of it and Lout duly told us what had gone on. But later that night I got a call from Leroy, who kept in touch even though he was still a Como. He told me that in fact he, Jock and the third Como hadn't been alone when they walked into the pub. He said Jock had the entire Comanchero club sitting up around the corner in a side street. He had a member standing out on the street watching the pub, and if one of them had stepped out and given the signal, the entire club was going to charge in.

We filled the club in on the details at the next meeting night, and on the following Saturday, club night, we left the old ladies at Louisa Road with a couple of prospects while we rode into Parramatta. We cruised around, revved the bikes, stopped at just about every pub there. Then we cruised up to the Royal Oak, where we spent a couple of hours. We didn't see a single Comanchero, but we'd done what we'd gone to do. We could make statements too.

ABOUT TWO weeks after the blue at the Bull & Bush, Snoddy called everyone and told us to come to the club-house. He had something important to say.

Once all the members had arrived, we gathered in the pool room where we held our meetings and Snoddy made his announcement. Jock had rung him to declare war on the club.

It might have been funny if it wasn't so serious.

Snoddy said he'd told Jock it was bullshit and that the two of them should just settle it between them, one on one.

Jock wouldn't be in it.

Snoddy had also offered him the option of the two sergeants fighting.

'You'd love that, wouldn't ya,' Jock had said. 'A punch-up man on man. You know you'd wipe us out. Nuh, this is going to be guerilla warfare. There's no rules. You won't know when we're going to hit you or where.'

Snoddy said Jock had continued to rattle on – 'You know I'm the supreme commander . . . We're not gunna stop till we wipe you out . . .' – until Snoddy got sick of it and hung up on him.

We spent the rest of the night talking about what Jock would do next. I thought he'd sit back and build up his club, taking in anybody on two wheels, and that he wouldn't strike until he had about fifty blokes. Others disagreed. I almost got myself killed finding out that they were right.

ABOUT THREE days after war was declared, I decided to go for a ride into Parramatta by myself to see if any Comos tried pulling me up. If they did, I was going to bash them and take their colours. Unfortunately, while I was out looking for them, I think they were out looking for me. I only got as far as Five Dock, about three kilometres from home, when a little white Jap car pulled up alongside me on Parramatta Road. I recognised Foghorn

and Sparra with another Como I'd never seen before. I
tried to pull ahead but all of a sudden they swerved at
me. I tried putting my leg out to stop their car hitting
the bike, but the bike went down and suddenly I was
underneath it, sliding along at a fair speed towards the
gutter, trying to hold the bike up so it didn't get too
badly damaged.

I was in big trouble, but it was my lucky day. I missed
the gutter and bounced up the driveway of a car yard
instead, the bike on top of me and petrol pouring from
the tank. I came to a stop and felt okay but I couldn't
lift the bike off. This dopey car salesman was standing
there with all these other dudes in suits: 'Are you hurt?'
Not one of the stupid pricks tried pulling the bike off. A
young bloke riding past on his pushy stopped and tried
to lift the bike off me. It was too heavy for him but he
took enough of the weight for me to leverage my leg
and push it off. I got it up onto its stand, grabbed the
car yard hose and washed the bike off before washing
myself down. I straightened the handlebars, checked the
bike, then got back on and rode home.

I was straight on the blower to Snoddy and told him
it was on. With that, Snoddy called a meeting. Everyone
turned up and I told them what had happened, warning
them to be careful.

Someone asked, 'D'ya think he's gunna keep going
like this? Will running you off the road even up for the
Bull & Bush?'

'The Bull & Bush was us evening up for Junior,'
Snoddy said. 'I think Jock'll carry on with it. But just
like when we were riding with him, he won't do nothing

himself. He'll send the others out to do the dirty work and he'll sit back in the clubhouse.'

Over the next few weeks the war intensified, and there was a lot of bashing. It was mainly us doing the bashings, though; Jock's lot tended to stick to trying to run us off the road in their cars and sneaking up on our clubhouse.

Bongo Snake was riding out at Rosehill on Parramatta Road, not far from their clubhouse, when Leroy in a ute and another carload of them ran him off the road. As with me, his bike ended up on top of him and they gave him a bit of a going-over with baseball bats. Then they did what most bikers would never do – they smashed his bike. Dumped it on top of him and left.

About four days after Bongo Snake was bashed, the back window of my car was shot out in the driveway alongside my house. To me, this was a real low act because it was at my home, endangering Donna and the kids.

The next day I rocked up to their clubhouse at Rosehill and banged on the door but there was no one there. I left a Bandit card with a message on the back that if anyone came near my home again the gloves'd be off and I'd be making house calls myself.

Then we got a visit from the cops. They had a warrant to search our clubhouse for guns. They said the Comanchero clubhouse had been shot up and we were their suspects. It was bullshit. We hadn't shot them up. They'd obviously done it themselves to set us up and have the cops confiscate any weapons we might have. We didn't even have any at the club. In those days, guns weren't a regular part of bike club life.

* * *

AROUND THIS time, Jock got knocked off his bike by a small truck. I always knew he was going to get into an accident because he had such bad night vision with those thick glasses.

This incident apparently happened in the late afternoon, early evening. For some reason, a couple of cars had broken down at a set of lights on Marsden Road just after he'd gone through, holding up all the traffic. Then another car broke down at the other end of the road. Where this truck came from I don't know. It just appeared, apparently. I always thought Jock probably just ran into it. But he seemed to think the truck had tried to run him over. If it had it would have saved a lot of problems, but whoever was driving the truck made the wrong decision and swerved around him.

IF ANY good was coming out of the war, it was that I was starting to see who the real hard-core blokes in the club were and who was just along for the ride. Take Davo for example. He took it upon himself to do what I'd done and go out to the Comos clubhouse to front Jock. He'd known Jock a long time and obviously thought he could talk some sense into him. Jock wasn't there but he fronted Leroy and Sunshine. When he came back and told me what he'd done I thought, While we've got staunch members like Davo, this club will keep going.

Through all this, Sheepskin and Leroy kept calling me on the phone to see how I was going. Sometimes I'd call them. We knew that if we ran into each other on the street it would be a punch-on because our clubs were at war, but on a personal level we were still friends.

Leroy and Sheepskin would keep me posted on what the Comos where up to. They never gave me any information that might have helped us beat them, but if there was something that they thought didn't really matter, or if they felt it was the right thing to do, they'd give me a tingle. They didn't like the way their club was going about the war. Equally, if some Comos got bashed they'd ring and ask me what the go was. It helped stop the two clubs really blowing up.

In one call I got from Leroy in August he told me that the whole club had been told to get me. He wasn't being threatening. Just letting me know.

He said that Jock had some T-shirts made up with my picture printed on them. On one batch there was a hammer pointed at my head with the words *Hammer Caesar*, and on the other batch there was a big nail going into my head with the words *Nail Caesar*.

Leroy also told me about a stunt the Comos pulled one Saturday night when we were out with our old ladies. He said that after we'd left the clubhouse for our club ride, the Comos had a car with a CB radio follow us to the pub. They waited until we left to return home and radioed ahead to Foghorn, who was parked in his ute with Snowy and some other blokes back at Louisa Road. Foghorn and Snowy then poured a forty-four gallon drum of diesel on the road where they knew we would come flying down the hill into a big sweeping left-hand turn. They were hoping to bring the whole club down on top of each other, old ladies and all. They didn't give a fuck if old ladies got hurt. As it turned out, we rode straight over it without even noticing.

The diesel plan wasn't a bad idea. I probably would

have done it myself if it had been only blokes that you
were going to take out. Leroy had a real soft spot for
Donna and didn't like the idea that she could have been
killed, which is why he told me about it.

Things were getting pretty nasty when one day Sheepskin rang. 'Can I come over to your place – without
getting bashed? There's something serious I need to talk
over with you. You've got no worries with me. You've
got me word. All I wanna do is talk.'

'Yeah, all right.'

So he came over and he had this tall, well-built bloke
with him who he introduced to me as his prospect,
Pappy.

'Ceese,' he said, getting straight down to business,
'I've left the Comos and Pappy's left with me.'

'Why?'

'I got put between a rock and a hard place.' He said
that Jock had come to him and told him that he had to
put a hit on me and a hit on Shadow. Sheepskin was
really close to both of us. He said he asked Jock why he
wanted me and Shadow bumped off rather than Snoddy.
'Snoddy's the president,' he'd said. 'Why wouldn't you
want him knocked off?'

Jock had said it was me who held the club together
and that if I went, the only one who'd step into my
spot would be Shadow. 'If we get rid of both of them,
the Band-Aids will fall to pieces.' They called us Band-
Aids.

'I didn't even have to think about it,' Sheepskin told
me. 'I was willing to get into a fist fight with youse for
the sake of the Comos but there's no way I was gunna
off ya. I've known youse too long. And anyway, I knew

211

if I missed the first time, there wouldn't be no second chance.' So Sheepskin said that he turned round to Jock and told him no way. If it was a choice between that or the club, he was leaving. So he left and Pappy went with him.

He said he and Leroy had been trying to end the war but he could see things were about to explode; Foghorn and Snowy were always in Jock's ear telling him how great he was, feeding his ego, and trying to egg him on to do more.

He admitted to me that the Comos had got a couple of prospects to shoot up their own clubhouse. They fired a few harmless shots into a garage door then Jock rang the cops to say the Bandidos had just driven past and shot at them.

Sheepskin got up to go. 'Anyway, I thought I'd just come over and tell ya so you can watch your back and you can let Shadow know that there's a contract out on him too.'

Pappy added, 'Sheepskin's right. You wanna watch your back. They've got these T-shirts out now with your face on 'em.'

I thanked Sheepskin for coming round. We shook hands and they hopped in the car and took off. I got on the blower to Shadow and told him about it. I said, 'I'm not gunna call a club meeting, I don't want to worry the brothers any more than I have to, but you tell Snoddy what Sheepskin had to say.'

'All right, Ceese, you watch your back.'

'You do the same.'

* * *

THINGS WERE building up and some of our blokes were getting restless. They didn't like the fact that at any time you could be run off the road. After our next club meeting, Shadow, Snoddy and I had an officers' meeting and we all agreed that if I could arrange it, I'd punch on with Leroy, or whoever they picked, and that the losing club would drop their colours. We knew that even if we won the fight, Jock wouldn't stick to the agreement, but we knew Leroy would and he had a lot of influence.

So I went to front Jock at their clubhouse, but he wasn't there. I spoke to Leroy and Sparra instead.

'Let's put an end to all this shit,' I said. 'Why don't we just punch on, you and me. You've always thought you could beat me, and I know I can beat you. The loser drops their colours.'

That stirred him right up like I knew it would.

'I'll take you on,' he said.

'There'll just be me and you and one other bloke from each club.'

'All right, I'll put it up to Jock.'

'Can't ya make the decision yourself? You're the sergeant-at-arms.'

'The Comos aren't run like you run the Bandits. I've gotta ask Jock.'

So he went away and got back to me a while later. Jock had said no way. It was guerilla warfare. And that was that.

BY THIS time, a lot of members had stopped riding their bikes and wearing their colours. It was just too dangerous. But I always rode my Harley-Davidson Wide Glide and wore my deck. I wasn't going to let anyone intimidate me. I was riding to the clubhouse the next Saturday with Donna on the back as usual, when we came down to the bay at Haberfield. As we approached the rowing club, I heard a couple of gunshots. A few moments later, I smelt petrol and felt a dampness on my leg.

I gunned the bike over a little bridge where the road went up the hill to Lilyfield, then pulled over. The right leg of my jeans was saturated in petrol. I looked at the tank and saw a bullet hole. It was a small calibre .22 or a .223. Luckily, I'd just filled up with petrol, so even though the bullet hit high up on the tank, it went through petrol. If I'd only had half a tank it would have gone through fumes and that would have been a lot more dangerous.

I leant the bike over and poured some petrol out of the tank onto the ground. Donna had some chewing gum which I stuck into the hole. 'From now on we'll have to go a different way to the clubhouse,' I said, kicking myself because I should have known it was a dangerous spot to ride through at night, with the bay on one side and the park on the other.

We got back on and rode to the clubhouse, where I got the bike into the garage and had a good look over her. That's when I got the biggest shock of the night – I found a bullet hole through the seat Donna had been sitting on. That freaked her out a bit and it wound me up something fierce.

I rode the bike home, grabbed an eight-shot pumpy, threw it in the boot of my old V8 XR Falcon and drove back to the clubhouse. I was spewing that they'd taken a shot at Donna. Dead set, if I'd run into any Como that night I would have blown his head off. Hang the consequences. If I'd run into six or seven of them, they were all going to the cemetery. And if there were fifteen and I had time to reload I would've done them too. If someone wants to go all the way with me, killing them doesn't worry me one bit.

Back at the clubhouse, everyone was on a short fuse, especially now they knew the Comos didn't give a fuck about whether your old ladies were with you or not. I said, 'You blokes should have known that from when they put the diesel on the road.'

I grabbed Snoddy and Shadow and said, 'I think a few of the fellas are losing a bit of heart. We're going to have to do something to gee them up a bit.' There were a few blokes who Snoddy and I thought were going to hand in their colours. He wanted to have a morale booster to make the blokes who were on the point of leaving think, 'Nah, this is too good a club to leave.'

'What if we bring the anniversary of the club forward?' I said. The club had started on 22 November and it was now only August, but we'd been at the Louisa Road clubhouse for twelve months and I thought it would really pick the guys up to have something to celebrate.

Snoddy said it was a good idea, and Shadow agreed. They left it up to me to arrange for a big cake to be made with *Bandidos Australia First Anniversary* written across it.

It worked a treat. When I brought the cake to the clubhouse the next meeting night and everyone saw it, they were rapt. Me and Snoddy held the knife together and cut the first slice. It was just what the brothers needed to lift their spirits. It had the right effect – although over time it created the mistaken idea that the club started in August 1983.

The real hard-core brothers in the club didn't need a cake to pep them up. You only had to look in their eyes. They always had the same look; nothing fazed them. I think a few of my brothers were even enjoying the war. I said to Kid Rotten, 'This is like an anniversary for you, it's nearly a year since you changed your name from Animal to Kid Rotten.'

Kid said, 'Well I didn't want anything that reminded me that I was a Como. Animal was my Como name.'

'Fair enough,' I said.

IN THE next couple of weeks it got pretty hairy. With all the shooting going on I put some barbed wire round the front of my house, mainly so that if the Comos decided to turn up en masse there was something to slow them down while I got Donna and the kids out the back door or into the back room which I'd reinforced with sandbags.

Back in them days, outlaw clubs didn't have guns around. There was a culture of stand-up toe-to-toe fighting. If you got thumped, you got thumped. People didn't try to square up with guns. And in all the time I'd been riding, I'd never known of anyone from an outlaw club going to the coppers until Jock called them on us. Things have changed now. It's gone from fists and knives to guns. And drive-bys on blokes' homes have become the norm.

But all this was very unusual back in 1984. I only

had that eight-shot pump-action shotgun because it had been offered to me at a good price. The only time I had ever had any reason to use it was when we went pig hunting. A couple of my brothers were right into the pig hunting. They'd go once every three months or so and I went with them a few times and just destroyed the pigs with this thing.

THE WAR had been escalating through August. On the twenty-fourth, Wack drove his car past a Como house. He didn't know it was a Como house, it was just a coincidence, but inside, someone recognised him. One of them followed Wack down to Shadow's place and went back to get the others.

Three carloads pulled up – led by Jock's brother-in-law, Glen Eaves – and let fly. There were bullets going through the front door and the windows. Shadow shot back and the Comos took off. Shadow and Wack then chased them through a few suburbs to someone's house. Shadow and Wack pulled up and told the Condoms to get out, threatening to punch their heads in. With that the Comos let fly again and Shadow ended up with a few bullet holes in his car. He headed home and found his old lady in a real mess. The cops were there and wanted to know what had happened.

Shadow just told them a couple of cars had pulled up out the front and the blokes in them had started shooting. He said when they took off he chased them but stopped when they started shooting at his car. The cop went over and looked at Shadow's car. 'You're mighty lucky.'

'Don't I know it,' Shadow said.

Shadow went inside and got on the blower to Snoddy and me. Snoddy was really upset because he and Shadow were as close as any two blokes could be. Snoddy called a special meeting and said that all this shit had to stop.

Afterwards, Mouth – the member whose vote I'd abstained from – called Snoddy, Shadow and me aside. Mouth said he'd been practising at the back of his property in Galston and reckoned he could put a bullet into the front wheel of a bike travelling at any speed. He suggested he take out Jock's front wheel and bring him down.

It sounded okay to me. 'I don't give a fuck if it's just Jock,' I said. 'But I'm not going to go along with it if they've got their old ladies with 'em.'

'Well they've been doing it to us,' he said.

'Just because they do it to us doesn't mean we have to sink as low as them.'

Snoddy agreed. 'If you can do it and there's no old ladies or kids involved, have a go.'

But funnily, when Mouth got the go-ahead, he suddenly decided it was a bad idea. As usual, he was all piss and wind.

'I don't think I could kill anyone,' he said.

'You get over it,' I said. 'It's only the first one that's hard.'

CHAPTER 13

Bernie was round at my place one day. 'You seemed really pissed off with Mouth, big fella,' he said.

'Well I never voted him into the club.'

I know you're supposed to love all your brothers in the club, but when you think about it, that's impossible. There's blokes that are good for the club, but you also get plastic gangsters that slip through and get their colours. They just want to prance around with a ton of gold round their neck and a gold ring on every finger. I reckon if you pulled their boots off they'd have them on their toes, too.

Bernie asked Donna if he could talk to me in private so she went out the back.

'What is it?' I asked.

'Well, I've been hearing some rumours about how Jock came off his bike.'

'Yeah?'

'I heard Snoddy and a couple of other members ran him off the road in some sort of ute.'

'Yeah, I've heard the rumour too. But don't you think if Snoddy had've done it he'd have got a semi, not a ute, and instead of sideswiping Jock he'd have run right over the top of him and turned him into porridge? I reckon it's just another rumour started by the Comos.'

'Yeah, you're probably right.'

I called Donna back inside and she said, 'Can I say something to both of you?'

'Yeah.'

'You know, it's not just me but all the old ladies in the club, we really worry about you guys. Like when you got run off the road, Ceese. When you came home I just saw the bike, and it reminded me of when John Boy got hit. I don't want to lose you that way.'

'Don't worry, I'm not going anywhere. It'd take a Mack truck to get rid of me.'

'Why do you reckon Jock really started this war?' Bernie asked.

I tossed it up but decided, Nah, I can't tell him the real reason. Instead I said it was probably because Jock, Foghorn and Snowy were always used to being big fish in a small pond, and as the club had gotten bigger they felt like they were losing their importance. Which had certainly contributed to the tension within the Comos. But to me, that was just a creation of their own insecurities. As far as I was concerned, Jock was the president and that was the way it was always going to be. Unfortunately, with Foghorn and Snowy in his ear he'd got it into his head that I was after his job. Nothing could have been further from the truth. It had taken him four hours just to talk me into being sergeant.

Donna said to Bernie, 'There were some really good times in the Comos.'

'Yeah I heard that,' Bernie said.

'The times I loved best were the runs,' she said. 'And Christmas. You know, Caesar used to buy every member and their old ladies a present every year. And he was the only one who did it. And then this year, after they fed all those homeless kids, he did exactly the same thing for the Bandidos. He gave 'em all a special present. That's how much the club and his brothers mean to Caesar.'

'Come on, woman,' I said. 'You're putting it on a bit thick.'

'You're always putting the club first,' she said. 'Like the way you're always last one out of the pub, making sure the members and their old ladies are out and okay. And whenever there's been a fight it's always you, Bull, Shadow, Wack, Snake and Chop right up the front. Youse do it because you don't want to see any of the brothers in the club get hurt. I'm getting a bit sick of you having to do everything for them.'

'Calm down,' I said.

She sat there and gave me a big smile. She knew she could wrap me round her little finger.

Donna went out to the kitchen while me and Bernie yakked on about our bikes and about Jock. Bernie and I had gotten pretty close after he came over from the Loners so I suppose he didn't feel funny asking the next question: 'Is it true what they say about you having a graveyard up in the Snowy Mountains?'

'What makes you ask that?'

'I've heard rumours since way back when I was a Loner, and since I've come over to the club, that when you were working for a bloke up the Cross you used to get rid of people by taking them down the Snowy.'

'Well that's for me to know and everyone else to find out.'

Bernie just laughed. 'I'll remember never to go skiing with ya.' Then he changed the subject. 'Did you hear about Kid and Davo last week?'

'What about 'em?'

'The three of us were up the Cross and we picked up this sheila, a real cute little blonde. She had a flat in Victoria Street so the three of us went back there. Talk about kinky, mate. She had us tie her up and Kid was right up her and at the same time she was giving Davo a head job. I was just standing back watching.'

'You mean waiting yer turn?'

'You're not wrong. She was a real goer. Best fuck I've had in a long time. We're arranging nine or ten of us to go up to her place next week. You wanna come?'

'Nah, I'm not interested. I'm happy with the one I've got.'

'Oh well, your misfortune.'

With that we walked out the front and Bernie showed me the new set of pipes he'd put on his bike. He started her up.

'Yeah, she sounds good,' I said.

'Anyway, I've gotta head off. I've got some tennis lessons to give.'

'It's hard to imagine a bloke who gives tennis lessons riding with an outlaw club,' I said.

'I don't tell anyone. I always rock up to the tennis courts in my car.'

'Well now, wouldn't the brothers like to hear this.'

'What?'

'You're ashamed to rock up at your place of work with your colours.'

'Come on, Ceese, you know what it's like over the north shore. If I was to rock up and they knew I belonged to the Bandits I'd never have any clients.'

'Well what'd you do when you were a Loner?'

'Same thing. Turn up in the car. No one over in the tennis club knows I'm in a bike club.'

'Well then I'd get a new job, 'cos if it was me I'd never work anywhere where I couldn't show me colours.'

SOON AFTER Bernie's visit, I got a call from my brother Shadow. He wanted me to come out to his place so I got on the bike and cruised over. Gloves was there in his training gear.

'I got you to come out so you could watch me and Gloves spar,' Shadow said. 'We've been doing it for weeks now on the quiet. You're the first one we've told.'

Since his brother Knuckles had been wiped out in the accident, Gloves had taken it upon himself to live up to the family's boxing potential; he was being trained by Kid for his big comeback fight. The war hadn't worried Gloves. He just took it in his stride and kept on training.

Shadow had the back of his place done up with heavy bags, a speed ball and weights. It was a great place for him to work out. So I watched Shadow and Gloves get into it, and even though Gloves was the professional, Shadow gave as good as he got. They sparred eight three-minute rounds, then had a break and got onto some more sparring.

'Shadow should take up boxing,' Gloves said to me afterwards. 'He's as good as any bloke I've fought.' Gloves had fought a lot of good boxers, too: the French champion, and a lot of amateur fighters before he turned professional. He'd won all his professional bouts.

Gloves's big comeback fight was scheduled for Friday night, 31 August 1984 – the day of my little fella Daniel's fourth birthday.

Everyone in the club was excited about going to watch it at the Marrickville RSL club. At the next club meeting, we all confirmed that we'd be there. Snoddy was the only one who couldn't make it. He was going pig shooting at Griffith, where he was going to be sussing out some blokes who were setting up a Bandidos chapter down there. But he said he'd be back by the Saturday night.

I asked all the fellas if they were still coming to Daniel's party on the Sunday. I'd brought it up at the meeting two weeks earlier. We figured that since Gloves's fight was on the Friday, we'd leave the Saturday to recover and have the party on the Sunday – Father's Day. Donna had arranged with the old ladies to get all the food together.

The brothers all said they'd be there. Then Mouth and Bongo Snake mentioned a swap meet out at a pub in Milperra called the Viking Tavern. They said it'd be a good spot for us to go for a ride while the sheilas were getting the party ready.

'Me and Snoddy had already thought about going for a ride out to the Caringbah Inn,' I said.

Lance stood up. 'I reckon the Viking Tavern would be the go.'

'That's because it's close to your place,' I said. 'And you just wanna buy some parts.'

'What's wrong with that?' he asked.

'Nothin'. I just reckon the Caringbah Inn would be a better ride. More people'd see us and they've got some good bands on of a Sunday.'

Mouth and Bongo Snake carried on something fierce about this swap meet and how it was going to be the best thing round.

'Yeah,' I said, 'but if we're meeting at Lance's, that's a ride of about three K. So where's the ride?'

'Oh, but, you know, it'll be great.'

'What bands are on?' I asked.

'Oh, there'll be bands there.'

'Who?'

They couldn't name any, but they just pushed and pushed to go to this thing. Later, I'd look back and wonder about them and why they wanted to go so badly. But anyway, the club took a vote and the majority wanted to go to the Viking Tavern. So that was the plan.

CHAPTER 14

Friday night came and just about the whole club was at the Marrickville RSL club to watch Glovesy. Nearly everybody had rocked up in cars because we weren't sure we'd get in wearing colours, and everyone wanted to see the fight. When Gloves's bout came up, he smashed the state champion and won the prize for the best fight of the night, so we all went back to the clubhouse and partied on. Glovesy was yahooing around and sparring. 'I'm gunna be champion of the world.'

The next night was club night. We were there with the old ladies and it was still all about how good Gloves had been, everyone congratulating him. We went for a ride to the Duke of Edinburgh at Pyrmont, had a few drinks in there, went for a run through the Cross to show off the colours, then headed back to the clubhouse. It was all good fun. Jock and his guerilla war was still on our minds, but if they wanted to attack us on a night when we were all together, that was going to be their problem.

I went home at one am, as per my arrangement with Shadow, who looked after the club till morning.

Next day, Father's Day, dawned like it was going to be a great one. After doing the usual family thing, about thirteen or fourteen of the brothers turned up at my place. All the old ladies were already there helping Donna fix things up for Daniel's party: blowing up balloons, putting lollies out for the kids, making salads. The tables were set up out the back. We got a spit going with a lamb on it, and had a pile of snags and chops ready to go on the barbie.

Unbeknown to the club, I'd bought one of the first Harley-Davidson Softails to come into the country. And I'd had the motor rebuilt to eighty-eight cubes by a mate of mine called Witch. I'd had Mac the Brush repaint it in a metallic black with a gold fleck, with red and yellow flames all over the tank and the guards. He'd done an immaculate job. While the brothers were in talking to their old ladies I went out to the garage; I thought I'd start her up and they'd all come running out when they heard the roar and get the surprise of their lives. So I pulled the cover off and softly tried kicking her over. Nothing happened. I tried again and again, kicking harder each time until after fifteen minutes I gave up. This is fuckin' great, I thought. This was going to be my big showpiece for the day. I didn't have time to fuck around with it all day, or worse, ask someone to try and fix it. I decided I'd fix her later then ride it over to the next meeting and surprise everyone then. As it turned out, I'd never sit on that bike again.

I rolled the Wide Glide out instead, went in and called everyone together. We told the old ladies we were going, got on our bikes and rode away from all the kids' lollies and balloons. There were no special farewells. We were only going to be gone for a couple of hours then be back for the party. As we pulled away we could see the old ladies and the kids – from babies up to eight- or nine-year-olds – out in the backyard, clearly visible from Frederick Street, one of the busiest roads in Sydney's innerwest. It was obvious we weren't expecting trouble otherwise we'd never have left them there.

The next time they'd see us would be on the news.

WE GOT to Lance's place at Pringle Street, Condell Park, and saw that Snoddy's Falcon station wagon was there. He'd been meant to return on the Saturday from his week of hunting and getting to know the blokes in Griffith. But they'd thrown him a party and he got sozzled so he ended up staying an extra night and then driving his station wagon the 550 kilometres from Griffith that morning straight to Lance's to meet us.

We went round the back of Lance's and put the bikes in his backyard where all the other brothers were. Lance had one of the biggest backyards you've ever seen. I walked down towards his garage where Junior was working on his bike, then headed over to Snoddy. 'I'm gunna go for a ride down the tavern and make sure there's no Comos down there,' I said.

'No need, Caesar,' he said. 'I've already sent Sleazy and Maverick.'

'How long ago?'

'About two hours.'

'Yeah, but anyone could have turned up in that time. Maverick and Sleazy wouldn't know what they were doin' anyway.'

'Look, we'll just get the bikes going and we'll head down there now. They won't turn up. In all the years I rode with Jock he's never gone to a bike show. He's too afraid someone might get friendly with another club.'

Shadow came over. 'What's going on?'

'I want to go down the tavern and make sure there's no Comos there,' I said. 'If there is, we'll all ride over to the Caringbah Inn instead. I don't wanna get into a blue in public.'

'Fuck it,' Shadow said. 'If they're there we'll just give 'em a floggin'.'

'Yeah,' said Snoddy.

'Look, I'm going down the tavern,' I said.

'Come on, Ceese,' Shadow said. 'Don't make a big thing of it.'

'Yeah,' Snoddy said. 'I'm the president and I'm telling ya we'll be leaving in about five minutes. Just stay here.'

Ha, I thought to myself, after all these months now he wants to make the decisions. So I went down to Junior. 'Is your bike ready?'

'Yep.' He tried kicking it over but it wouldn't start. Snoddy yelled out to Junior, 'You've got fifteen minutes. If it don't start you're going in one of the cars.'

But Junior got it going and all the bikes pulled out the front of Lance's, lined up down the street. We were just waiting for Snoddy and Lard to get into Snoddy's station wagon – still loaded with all his camping gear – and for

Bull, Shadow and Wack to get into Bull's Holden wagon. The only members that were missing were Bongo Snake and Mouth.

All the bikes started up. I was out in front with a baseball bat strapped to my handlebars in case of trouble. The two cars were in the middle. We headed towards the Viking Tavern.

Once we reached Milperra, Snoddy and Bull's station wagons pulled out of the pack and went to the front. Snoddy's Falcon was first into the driveway of the sprawling ranch-style pub, followed by Bull's Holden, then me.

They turned right into one of the car park rows shaded by skinny gum trees, but there were no spots to stop. The place was crowded with people and stalls. The smell of barbecuing meat filled the air.

Snoddy and Bull drove slowly up the parking row until a car pulled out in front of Snoddy, blocking his way. I looked back to check on the rest of the blokes and I saw that they were all in the car park. That's when I noticed the first sign of trouble.

Jock's sidekick, Foghorn, was driving in behind us in his ute. He stopped, blocking our way out. I watched him get out of the ute carrying an M1 carbine – the American World War II semi-automatic – and run into the crowd towards the pub.

I looked down and saw a bunch of Comancheros standing about three parking rows away. They all had shotguns on their hips. I saw Leroy, who had become their sergeant-at-arms, among them. I looked around for Jock but couldn't see him. I figured that, as usual, he'd sent his blokes out while he stayed back at the clubhouse.

There was no time to think. We weren't ready for a gun battle. And we were trapped. I knew if we tried to walk or run out of the car park, we were all going to get shot in the back. I think they expected that when we turned up and saw all the guns we'd go to water, panic and throw our colours down or whatever. They'd obviously forgotten who they were dealing with.

I got off my bike and started walking straight towards them without bothering to get the bat off my handlebars. I just strode down between the rows of parked cars, yelling: 'Put down your guns and fight like men.' I thought that if I could just get to Leroy he'd probably put down his shotty and have a go at me, one on one. The other thing flashing through my head was that the closer I got to them, the better chance I had of grabbing a couple of them and snatching their guns. That way, if anyone started shooting I had something to shoot back with.

I was about one car away from Leroy when I challenged him directly.

'You really want to go one on one?' he said.

'Yeah, put down your gun and let's do it. If you win, we'll drop our colours. If I win, youse drop your colours and that's the end of the war.'

'You're on.'

Leroy was a big boy, and super strong. A real hard bloke. He put his shotgun down against the car and shaped up.

I thought I was alone, but then I looked back over my right shoulder and there were my brothers, Shadow, Chop, Bull, Snake and Wack, along with Davo, Gloves, Roach, Lance and Zorba, all spread in a line just behind me. Bear was running towards us. They'd all come down to back me up and I felt this intense pride. None of us had a gun. This was what it was all about: punching on when the odds were against you.

Then I realised that they were the only ones there. The rest of the club had either stayed back with the cars or run out into the street.

I looked back at Leroy. Standing just behind him was a Como by the name of Hennessey, shaking like a leaf, his gun still at his hip. I thought, This bloke's gunna be a real worry. He was staring at my brother Snake, and Snake was calling him all the names under the sun. I knew this Hennessey didn't *want* to start shooting, but that he just might because he was so scared of Snake.

Snake said something like, 'Put the gun down if you're not gunna use it. If you're gunna use it, use it.'

The next thing I knew, there was a bang and Snake went down. He'd been hit in the gut. Snake sat there with his hands over the wound, blood spurting out of his stomach.

I went cold.

I heard Snoddy, still up at his station wagon, calling Chop and Shadow to come back up and join him. Snoddy had to get round the back of his car and throw all his camping gear out to get to the only two guns we had – his two pig-shooting guns, a .357 carbine and a shotgun – and the ammunition.

Back down where I was, Leroy picked up his gun and ran behind a car. Straight in front of me in a tight little group were Sparra, Tonka and Snowy, all with shotguns hanging by their sides. They started to raise them, so I charged. I got my left arm wrapped around the barrels of their guns and had them pointed at the ground while I barged the three of them back onto the front of a car, pinning them down with my body. I was really giving it to Tonka while holding the other two down. Tonka hit the deck and I stomped on his chest and head with my Johnny Reb boots, crushing one side of his skull. I did everything I could to get him out of it until he went limp. Then, still holding Sparra down, I started belting in on Snowy with my elbow. He fell to the ground, soft as, unconscious.

That left just me and Sparra. With my left hand still pinning down the shotty in his right hand, he started throwing punches with his left. I used my spare hand to grab him by the throat. I tried to go for the vagus nerve on the side of his neck. If you know the right spot you can knock a man out or kill him by hitting the vagus nerve.

I looked over my shoulder and saw Snake sitting there holding his guts in, blood pouring through his hands. Leroy was standing over the top of him, his shotgun pointing down at Snake's head like he was about to finish him off.

I zoned out. The world went red. I gripped harder into Sparra's neck. I felt the shotty drop out of his hand and I squeezed harder. I felt my fingers ripping his skin. I saw blood coming out, and felt my fingers go still deeper into his flesh. I felt the side of his neck rip away as he hit the ground screaming.

I looked up and saw sneaky little Glen Eaves, Jock's brother-in-law, a tiny bloke with a real big mouth when he had a lot of blokes around him. He'd been in the army and he was lying on the ground in a firing position, pointing the shotty at me. For some reason, I think to get a better shot at me, he tried to get up onto his knees. But as he tried getting off the ground, he stumbled and the shotgun discharged into the ground near Sparra. I saw Sparra jerk, so I figured something had hit him. When they later took him away and did the autopsies, they found the wadding from a shotgun cartridge in his neck and concluded he'd been killed by the shotgun – but only after half his neck had been ripped out.

Once the shooting started it came from everywhere. All I could hear was gunshots but with all the rows of parked cars it was impossible to see where they were coming from. I looked around: there were Como colours climbing the back fence out of the car park, a bunch of them jumping into a green XY Falcon and heading for the bottle shop entrance. They took the door off the bottle-o they were trying to get out of the car park that quick. Most of the Bandidos who'd come down with me had got back to Snoddy and Bull's station wagons by this stage.

Snake was still sitting there with the blood spurting out between his fingers. My only thought was to get to him, and anyone who got in my way was a dead man. I took a step towards him. I saw Bull had this really huge Como down at the front of his car, kicking the shit out of him while the bloke tried to crawl under the car.

A Como came towards me and I grabbed him by the hair and started laying in. Davo was standing alongside me fighting another Como I'd never seen before. He was a real good bluer, Davo. He'd just finished this bloke off when I saw another Como coming up behind him with a bowie knife. I had my hands full so all I could do was yell out to Davo. He turned around just in time. Instead of getting it in the middle of the back, he got it up under his arm. Didn't that get him started. He beat the shit out of the bloke.

I finished with the bloke who'd just come at me and took another step towards Snake when for some reason I turned to my left. *Bang.* I felt it in the right shoulder. I staggered back a metre and it felt like I'd been hit by a baseball bat. I didn't know what it was at that point, I was stunned. It was a funny feeling. I always figured that if you got shot with a serious weapon, you'd get this burning, hot feeling, all the stuff you see in the movies. But it wasn't like that, it was just like getting hit with a baseball bat. I'd been hit with a .22 before but that was more like a little pin prick; .22s aren't much use to you unless you're actually standing up alongside the bloke and you got the barrel pointed just in under the ear. That's the best spot to put it.

I realised I'd been hit by a shotgun when I saw blood spurting out of lots of holes. My arm went numb.

Then I felt another thud – this time to my chest. It was like I'd been hit with another baseball bat but this time I knew straightaway that I'd been shot. Blood spurted out of my arm and my chest and into my face. It was suddenly hard to breathe. I coughed and blood came out.

I think I went down on one knee because I was bent over when a Como by the name of Alan came at me with a baseball bat or an iron bar and – w*hack* – he hit me on the side of the head, which I didn't like.

I just went *whooshka*, swung my hand out and caught him right in the nuts. He hit the ground alongside me and I grabbed him by the throat. I tried to rip his throat out, and I don't know if it was from being shot or what, because my wounds were on my right side, but I just couldn't get enough power into my left hand to do it.

I got to my feet, took the iron bar off him and hit him with it, then put the heel of my boot into his mouth. His teeth went everywhere and I started stomping on his head.

I could hear Chop and Shadow, about twenty feet off to my right, yelling, 'Bandidos! Bandidos!' It's a sound I'll always remember. They just seemed to keep yelling out, and even though I'd been shot twice, hearing my brothers yelling gave me strength.

LANCE AND Zorba were over bashing some Comos, Glovesy was still giving it to someone. I looked up and I was hoping to see the rest of the club come screaming towards us because I knew if the lot of us had gone these blokes we'd have run over the top of them. But it didn't happen.

I saw the Como JJ and his old lady down between two cars looking up at me pointing a handgun. To tell the truth, I can't remember whether it was JJ or his old lady with the gun because I had blood spurting into my eyes and I was feeling real dizzy, but knowing JJ it was probably his old lady. She had more balls than he did. I was looking down there through this haze and then all of a sudden *whack*, I was hit in the forehead. I didn't think I'd been shot; I just felt this thud and then this burning sensation and blood was in my eyes. I was staggering around blind, but I heard a voice. It was Bull.

'Get out of here, Ceese!' I wiped my eyes and saw Bull and Wack heading towards Snake.

I started finding it really hard to breathe. I'm gunna pass out, I thought. I didn't want to pass out down where the Comos were so I turned round and started to walk up the gentle slope to the street where the other half of the club were.

I looked up to Snoddy's Falcon about ten metres away and saw him leaning out of it, shooting towards the Comos who were about ten metres behind me. There was Chop and Shadow standing out in the open back where I'd been, just a couple of metres from the Comos, firing away and screaming to the other Bandits to get up to the street.

As I was walking up, I felt w*hack*, w*hack*, *whack*, little stings in the back. I knew from experience that they were probably .22s but I didn't know what was going on. It was too hard to see through the blood.

'Fuck it.' I stopped to turn around and go back down there to kill as many of them as I could before dying. Then something inside me said, No. Walk out. So I turned around again and staggered back up to the left and out of the direct crossfire.

My right leg was dragging behind and I couldn't feel my right arm. I was having trouble breathing but I just kept going and made it to the road. I saw all these Bandits up there.

Knuckles came up and grabbed me under the left arm. Kid, Lout and Bernie came over. Someone yelled to Hookie to come and help me. One of them waved down a car and it turned out to be this sheila who knocked around the club, Big Sue. Lout, Hookie and Bernie threw me into the back of her green Holden and I remember the car moving and seeing red and I was playing the last few minutes over in my mind. The numbness turned to pain. I remember Lout saying, 'We've got to get him to the hospital,' and hearing sirens.

Suddenly, someone was helping me up a hospital driveway and leaving me there on the ground outside. Later I found out that one of them had run over and rung the bell to emergency and the nurses had come out and found me lying there.

I was helped through some glass doors and now there were nurses all around me. I was on a bed or a table.

I was the first person from the tavern to reach the hospital. I could hear on the radio that they'd interrupted the regular programming to report a bikie shooting in Milperra. The doctor who was working on me said, 'What's going on down there?'

I was thinking, 'Fuckin' just fix me up.' The pain was getting worse.

The nurses tried to make me as comfortable as possible, but the doctor was trying to get my colours off me.

'You're not having me colours,' I said.

'You've got to take them off so I can examine you.'

There was no way anyone was getting my colours. I'd been shot. I'd seen my brother shot. I'd smashed and probably killed one bloke by ripping half his throat out. All for these colours. There was no way they were coming off.

'I've got to examine you,' he said. There was a running argument for about five minutes and I took a swipe at him. 'My colours stay here.'

'You'll die if we can't get them off.'

I had my left hand over my chest holding the vest under my right arm so they couldn't take it. Some wardsmen came in and they had enough blokes to hold me down. They cut the vest up the right-hand side and along the top of the shoulder so they could slip it off.

I heard the doctor say, 'We've got to stem the flow of blood from his head.' Something sharp got stuck into my head, then the doctor was pulling at something in my forehead. 'Does this look like a bullet to you?' I heard the doctor asking the nurse.

'Yes.' It turned out that JJ or his old lady had shot me in the head with what they said was a .38, which miraculously just lodged in my skull without penetrating.

Then the quack yelled out to a nurse that my lung had deflated. He grabbed a rod about a foot long with a thread on it like a self-tapping screw. He came up to me and thumped it in under my right arm, and started more or less screwing it in through the side of my chest. All of a sudden I took a deep breath, and that's the last thing I remember.

CHAPTER 15

I was waking up and dozing off. All I can remember is lights, a frigging lot of pain and Donna's face. Sometimes Mum was there too. I remember Mum sitting next to me holding my hand. She gave me a big hug and told me that she loved me. Then I went unconscious again. And there was always this bloke's face appearing in front of me. I couldn't work out who he was.

When I came to, they told me I was in intensive care and that I'd been out of it for a month. I asked about my brothers. Donna told me Snake and Wack were in a ward upstairs, but that was all she said. I saw three coppers standing just inside the door. Donna said they'd been there the whole time.

I felt like I had to see my brothers. I told the nurse that I wanted to go up to their ward but she said, no, I had to stay down here a bit longer.

'Take me up or I'll walk up meself. I'll crawl if I have to.' I started pulling tubes out of myself and tried to get out of the bed.

'Calm down,' the nurse said, 'all right. It will take me a few hours, but I'll get you up to the ward with your brothers.'

She came good on her promise and they wheeled me in my bed up to a room where Lard and Snake were. I was that glad to see Snake had survived the shot to the belly. He told me that Davo had just left, having recovered from his stab wound under the armpit.

I saw Donna having a big confab with a doctor. She came over with tears in her eyes and I thought, This isn't gunna be good. I'm gunna lose an arm or a leg or some bloody thing. She sat down beside me. 'Do you remember what I told you down in intensive care?' she asked.

'I don't remember anything from there.' She pulled the curtain round. 'I don't know how to tell you this.'

'What?'

'Shadow and Chop are dead.' She started crying. I put my left arm around her and just lay there. I couldn't believe it. Two of my brothers were gone.

Donna stopped crying. 'Are you all right?' she asked.

'No . . . Would you mind going, and letting me talk to Snake?'

'I'll wait out in the corridor.' She pulled the curtain back so I could see my brother.

'Do you know?' I asked Snake.

'Yeah, I knew on the day. Did Donna just tell ya?'

'Yeah.'

'I know how you're feeling.'

'Sorry, brother,' Lard said from the other side of the room.

There was an empty bed next to mine. 'Where's Wack?' I'd been told Wack was in this ward. It turned out he was in the room across the corridor, so I hit the buzzer to get the nurses in.

'Is me brother over in that room?'

'Yes.'

'Well bring him in here and put him in that bed.' Wack was the youngest of the Campbell brothers – except for Chrissy – and I thought it was important that we be together. He'd had part of his arm blown away and the remainder was sewn to his chest through a skin graft. After a bit of arguing and carrying on, they got Wack and put him in the bed alongside me.

I just couldn't take the news in. I was shattered. The worst day of my life was when my father died. That was the first time I'd ever shed a tear. This was the second time.

Wack started telling me what he knew. Apparently the Comancheros had turned up at the Viking Tavern at least twenty minutes before us and had been running round with shotguns and walkie-talkies while Jock swanned around with a machete in his hand playing the king dick. I don't know how they knew we were planning a trip to the Viking that day. Jock never went to bike shows.

Wack said that when we'd first rocked up to the tavern, he was with Bull and they walked down towards the Comos after me. As he was following me, he saw a heap of Bandits running out of the car park and onto the street. I really would've thought the whole club would be down there punching on. And if they had been, I don't think there would've been anyone killed because the Comos would have dropped their bundle and run.

Wack said that when the shooting started there was only Snoddy's shotgun and the .357 carbine. That was all we had. But Snoddy had called Wack and some of the other fellas who'd been punching on back up to the car, and on their way up some of them had picked up shotties that had been dropped by the Comos. So we ended up with a couple more guns and Snoddy had spare ammo in his station wagon from the hunting trip.

Shadow and Chop had each grabbed a shotgun and ammunition off Comos and started blasting away, but they'd been stuck deep on the Comos' side of no-man's-land. Shadow was killed by a single shotgun pellet in the throat. Chop had six pellets go through his chest. Wack had been shot standing up at Snoddy's car.

I asked Wack whether he'd seen Jock during the fight, because I hadn't.

'After you headed off up to the street there was a lull in the shooting and some of the Comos started yelling out, "Caesar's gone! Caesar's gone!" Then Jock came running out from behind the pub waving a machete above his head yelling, "Kill 'em all! Kill 'em all!"'

Jock later claimed that he'd been around the back of the pub and hadn't heard the shooting. As if.

Wack continued with the story. He said Lard ran down towards Jock with a pick handle and that's when he got shot in the foot. Snoddy started shooting at Jock so Jock ran back into the cars. Snoddy kept saying, 'Fuck! I've only got rabbit shot left.'

'The way he's running that's what you need,' Wack answered.

Wack remembered seeing Jock drop his machete then bend over to pick it up, facing up towards the car. Snoddy said, 'Fuck the old prick.' And shot him. Jock went down.

Snoddy was frantically searching for more slugs to put in the shotgun. He found a couple on the floor and loaded the shotty with them. 'This is it,' he said to Wack. 'The old cunt's dead.'

Snoddy was lining up the kill shot to the top of Jock's head when Bear came down to see if he could help any of the blokes that were round Snoddy's station wagon get out of the car park. When he saw Snoddy taking aim at Jock, he pushed Snoddy's arm to the side. Snoddy fired but missed by a couple of feet. Snoddy pumped it again and fired down towards Jock but couldn't get a good shot at him because Bear still had hold of the gun.

'What are you fuckin' doing, Bear?' Snoddy yelled.

'C'mon, Snoddy. There's been enough killing,' Bear replied.

Snoddy told Bear to fuck off. Bear headed back up to the street and Snoddy reloaded the gun with the rabbit shot to have another go at Jock, but by this time some of the Comos had dragged him behind a car and Snoddy couldn't get a good shot at him.

Wack said, 'But I'll give Snoddy this. From the time we got there till the time the coppers arrived, he never left that car. He just kept firing. Even after Chop and Shadow were hit. It just seemed to make him worse. He just wanted to shoot everything that had Como colours.'

Wack told me that four Comos had died in the fighting: Sparra (the bloke whose throat I'd ripped out), Foghorn, Dog and Leroy. I was really sorry to hear about Leroy. I said that the biker world had lost a good bloke. A lot of the blokes in the club wouldn't understand that, but he was a top fella.

Snake told me that after he'd been shot and the whole shitfight had erupted, Leroy had stood over him with his gun pointed at his head. Snake told Leroy, 'Well if you're gunna shoot me, fuckin' do it.' And Leroy had said, 'Not today, Snake. You're me brother. We'll get into it another day.' And with that he'd walked off and started shooting at other Bandits up in the car park.

'I just wish fuckin' Leroy and I had punched on and none of this had happened,' I said.

'Don't blame yourself, Ceese,' Wack said. 'It's that old cunt Jock's fault, not yours.'

'Wack, it's always been my job to look after you guys and the club.'

Wack reckoned that the only Como with any guts was one of their new blokes, Sunshine. 'After Jock was shot and I was there with part of me arm blown off, Bull stood up and yelled out to him, "How 'bout you let us get our wounded out, and we'll let youse get yours out." Sunshine agreed and so we went down and pulled everyone who was hurt up onto the road.'

Someone checked Chop but found that he was dead. Bull was getting Shadow out of the car park when the Comos started shooting again. Sunshine yelled at his fellow Comos to stop the shooting, which they did, and Bull was able to get Shadow out.

I didn't really want to hear the details of what had

happened to Shadow. It was upsetting Wack, too, because he'd seen it happen. But the one it had the biggest effect on was Bull, because Shadow was still alive when Bull got him out of the car park. Bull had tried to keep him going, but Shadow just died in his arms. So even though Bull wasn't shot, he probably had the worst time of it out of all us brothers.

Wack said it took a whole heap of Bandits to stop Bull going back into the car park to try and get Chop's body out from deep down in the Como's territory. A bunch of them grabbed him and told him that Chop had gone and he'd only get himself killed.

After that, the battle turned into a standoff. They shot at us a few times and we shot at them but the killing was over.

Wack said, 'When we got up onto the street, Snoddy got all the blokes together. He was really going off at the ones who didn't go down and punch on. But then he looked over and saw Bull laying over Shadow's body and he started to choke up and walked off by himself. Then the ambulance blokes rocked up. We let them in, so did Sunshine. Then some coppers. One copper went down and got Sunshine's shotty off him and that was kind of the end of it. A heap of coppers rocked up and they were going around quietening everybody. They took the guns and told us to stay where we were.'

There was so much confusion and so many people around, that any of the blokes could've just taken their colours off and walked away. They would never have been arrested. But the loyalty in the club was that strong that nobody left – except the three who had already taken me to hospital. (Hookie, Bernie and Lout went to

Lance's house and watched the rest of the blue on TV.)
There were still blokes with minor wounds, like Lard,
who was shot in the foot backing out towards the street
shortly before the ceasefire, and Porky, who'd been shot
in the leg. Others had been hit with baseball bats and
that. I would have been dirty on them if they'd left
because I know if it had been me, I would have stayed
till I saw the last bloke taken to hospital.

Wack said the ambulance rushed him to Bankstown
hospital. 'They took me into surgery and this one doctor
wanted to cut me arm off, but lucky for me they had a
visiting specialist there and he said to the other quack,
"We can save this young man's arm." So they put me
under and when I came to, me arm was sewn to me
stomach. That's all I sort of remember.'

I lay there for the rest of the day thinking about
Chop and Shadow until a nurse stuck something into
me and I passed out.

I BLACKED out for a few days and when I woke up I
noticed that Lard, in a bed across from me, had a
bandage around his foot. He told me a bullet had shattered it and they'd had to put a dirty great pin in it
to hold it together. In the bed next to him was Porky,
who'd moved into Snake's bed after Snake had been
discharged.

Porky had been shot in the leg. They had it in a
brace weighted down with a sandbag. He told me that
after he'd been shot, he was trying to crawl out of the
car park when he saw a Como lying there, trying to get
up. He saw an iron bar so he crawled over to it, picked

it up, crawled back to this Como and started bashing him. Then he got helped up to the street.

As for me, I was told I'd had four shotgun pellets go through my right lung and out my back. Four others had stayed in my back. I'd had thirty-three pellets inside me and the surgeons had managed to get more than twenty of them out.

I had tubes coming out of me everywhere. I'd developed an infection from the wounds in my lung and had a massive fever, so they had fans on me with big trays of ice in front of the fans to keep the fever down. At some stage a bloke came into the room and started talking to me like he knew me. I thought, 'Hang on, you're gay.' And he was.

'Do you remember me?' he asked. I just looked at him suspiciously. 'Come on, big fella, you gotta remember me.'

Fuck me roan, I thought, this bloke's trying to crack on to me.

Turned out he was the main nurse down in intensive care who'd been looking after me. It was his face that had kept fading in and out of my dreams when I was down there.

Then this other nurse came in. She was tall with long red hair. A real good looker. Lard was looking at me: 'You oughta thank her.'

'What for?'

'You'd be dead if it wasn't for her.' Lard turned to her. 'Hey, Ginger, tell Caesar what happened when you found him.'

She said she'd been called into work to help with the influx of casualties on the day. As she walked down the hallway towards emergency, she noticed a dead body on a trolley with a sheet pulled up over it. But then she saw the sheet twitch. She looked more closely and saw an arm hanging out and it twitched too. So she said she pulled the sheet back and went searching for a pulse. She found one then wheeled me back into emergency. 'Who put this bloke in the hallway?' she yelled.

No one owned up.

'Well whoever did, he's not dead.'

She told us how the doctor who'd pronounced me dead came running over and then I ended up in theatre and they pulled a few slugs out of my chest.

'Thanks, Sister,' I said.

'Don't worry about it,' she said, 'and call me Ginger.' Her friends reckoned she looked like that sheila on *Gilligan's Island*.

Ginger explained that the doctor who first worked on me had lost my pulse and couldn't pick up any breathing so he'd declared me dead. By that time, other wounded had started coming in so I got wheeled into the hallway.

'You must have died but somehow kick-started yourself again. It just wasn't your time to go. We were all amazed considering the gunshot wounds you had.'

After she'd gone, Lard said to me, 'If that quack ever comes back up here I'm gunna bash him.'

DONNA VISITED every day. Then she'd leave to check on the kids and come back of a night. My mum was there a lot too, even though her health wasn't the best. Lard and Porky had their visitors as well. Every time a visitor came, the cops searched their bags and put them through the rigmarole.

There were nine coppers on watch outside the room. We were told it was for our protection. We weren't under arrest. We hadn't been charged. They obviously thought we were even in danger in the toilets because they used to follow us in there.

The coppers would do a patrol through the room and go out onto the verandah. A couple of them would stand out there, have a smoke, then come back and sit on chairs just outside the door. They also had their own room with a television and lounge chairs where they sat for most of the day.

Most of the coppers weren't too bad. When our old ladies or relatives came, they didn't hassle them too much. But then we ended up with this bloody crown sergeant and he thought he was just it. Every time one of our old ladies turned up, he wanted to search them. I got sick of it so I yelled out to him one day, 'You ever put a hand on my old lady I'll rip your fuckin' throat out, in bed or not.'

He told me I wasn't as tough as I thought I was. And I said, 'Well come over here and we'll find out.' He left the room. Later that day an inspector turned up. I had a word with him and I told him about this crown sergeant. I said if he kept him there, there was going to be a blue. 'I don't care if I get thumped, I'm gunna have a go at him.' This inspector was a pretty good bloke. He walked out and went into their little room and I heard him telling the coppers off, saying they had to give us a bit of leeway. After that, all our old ladies had to do was open their bags to show they weren't bringing in guns or whatever, and they were allowed to stay as long as they wanted.

In the quieter times the cops would come in and chat. Mostly, they just wanted to know what it was like being a biker, especially the female cops. They wanted to know if the things they heard about what bikers did to women were true. Porky and Lard had a bit of a time bullshitting them but I played it pretty straight. One of them was a sergeant called Cathy. She was a good sort with a long blonde ponytail. She'd sit on the edge of my bed and talk to me for hours. Like most women, she seemed fascinated by the whole biker thing. She asked did we rape sheilas and what was 'pulling a train'. I told her that pulling a train was the same as an onion, when a sheila just lays back and takes everyone that's there. I told her that we didn't rape sheilas but that the trains did happen, although I never went in them.

She must have told the other cop sheilas because in coming days I had others sit down wanting to know things. They didn't seem to be grilling me for intelligence. It was all female stuff. They wanted to know about the wings, which were a little patch some bikers wore on their vests. I told them the Bandidos and Comos didn't have wings but a lot of other clubs did and that all outlaw bikers knew what they meant. The most popular ones were the red wings, for someone who's gone down and licked out a sheila who's got her monthlies. Then there were the brown ones – same sort of thing. You get the picture. Gold ones were for rooting a cop sheila and they seemed very interested in that one.

CHAPTER 16

One afternoon we heard the thunder of bikes pulling up outside. Then we heard the coppers in the corridor saying, 'You can't come in.'

'Try and stop us.' I recognised Davo's voice. Then all the Bandits just pushed past the coppers and came in. They were there for about half an hour. It was great to see everyone, but the coppers had called for back-up so Snoddy decided it would be better if the blokes left rather than cause a disturbance. Snoddy asked the coppers if just he could stay because he wanted to talk to me. They agreed. All the fellas went downstairs and Snoddy came over and pulled the curtains around my bed. I had a good idea what he was going to say. I could see tears developing in his eyes. 'I'm so sorry about what happened to Chop and Shadow.'

'I know you are, Snoddy.'

'If only I'd listened to you back at Lance's they wouldn't be dead and you and the other brothers wouldn't be here.'

'Well it's too late to change that.'

'But can ya forgive me?'

'Snoddy, there's nothin' to forgive. If anyone's to blame it's me for not standin' me ground and I'll regret it to the day I die.'

'Whaddya mean?'

'I knew I should have gone to the tavern and checked it out but I let you and Shadow talk me out of it. Any other time I wouldna done that. You know the club's safety always comes first with me, and I've never let anyone talk me out of what I've thought was the right thing to do for the club.'

Snoddy took my hand and put something in it. I looked down and it was the Campbell ring. 'I don't deserve it, Ceese.' I just shut my hand on it and we looked at each other.

'I heard you nearly got Jock,' I said.

'Yeah, if it hadn't been for fuckin' Bear the old cunt'd be dead.'

'Yeah, Wack told me about it.'

Lard or Porky had also told me that a fourteen-year-old girl, Leanne Walters, had been caught in the crossfire. Snoddy knew more of what had happened. He said Jock's good buddy Kraut had been running and Snoddy was following Kraut through the sights of the carbine. Snoddy didn't realise it, but Kraut was heading towards the girl. Snoddy fired from forty metres and the bullet went through Kraut's arm and deflected off some bone – he had a massive wound to his arm – and hit the girl. Snoddy said it was the worst thing that he'd ever done. The young girl had died.

'Well, where do we go from here?' he asked. 'Do you want me to resign?'

'No. There's no one else out there to run the club. You've gotta pull 'em together. Just remember the cops aren't gunna let this go. They'll be trying to bust everyone they can.'

'Well, no Bandits made a statement. But we were kept there all night, and I know for a fact that all the Comos made statements and signed them.'

'Fuckin' scumbags. I s'pose they thought they were giving us up by signing the statements. Just tell the brothers to keep their mouths shut and not to sign a thing.'

'Don't worry, I've already done that. Is there anything I can do for you and your family? What about your mum?'

'You can look in on her and keep an eye on Donna. She's taking it real hard. She was real close to Shadow and won't ask for help even when she needs it. If she needs anything make sure she gets it.'

'Always.'

'Donna tells me that Joanne's been going out partying even though Shadow's only been dead a month.'

'Well I didn't like to say anything, but she's been going out a bit with Mouth. I think it's just to keep her mind off things. But her mind should still be on Shadow.'

'I don't think Mouth'd try anything. But just make sure no one puts it on her. You know how Shadow would feel about that.'

'Don't worry, Ceese, no one from the club will go near her. I'll put the word out that no one's to touch her.'

'Thanks, Snoddy.'

'You sure there's nothing I can do for you right now?'

'No.'

'Maybe one day I can earn the ring back.'

'Maybe one day you can. Look after yourself, Snoddy, and most of all, look after the brothers.'

'I will.'

With that he went over and had a few words with Porky, then Lard, then Wack. He walked out and it was the last time I ever saw him.

Afterwards, Wack said to me, 'I heard you talking about the ring, and that one day he might get it back. You're gunna give it back to him, aren't ya?'

'Course I am, but I think Snoddy in his own mind needed to hand it back. I think he wanted to be punished for what happened to Shadow and Chop. It's like I told him, I don't blame him, but I wasn't gunna tell him he did nothing wrong, and make him take the ring back. When I get out of here he should've settled down and I'll give it back to him then.'

As usual Donna came in that night. I asked her how the kids were. She said that Daniel and Lacey were all right. They were too young to know what was going on. But Lee and Chane were copping a hard time at school, and so were Peggy and Samantha. 'The other kids and a lot of the teachers are giving them a real hard time over you being one of the main people mentioned in the papers.'

'Yeah that'd be right,' I said. 'The teachers'll change their tune when I get out . . . Where are our kids now?'

Donna said our good friends Cheryl and Pancho were looking after Daniel and Lacey. 'They've been really good, especially Cheryl. I don't know what I would've done without her help.'

'Yeah, she's always been a top chick.'

Me and Donna talked for a while. A copper poked his head in the door and said, 'I think it's time for visitors to leave.' Donna gave me a big tonguey and left.

ONE MORNING I heard some noise out in the corridor. This young copper came in and said to me, 'There's a huge Hells Angel out here who wants to see you, Caesar.'

'Is his name Guitar?' I asked.

'That's right.'

'Well let him in,' I said.

But the crown sergeant came in and said we weren't allowed visitors from another club. Guitar left without a fuss.

Another time I got a basket with some fruit, a bottle of wine and a get-well card sent by Sy from Lone Wolf. They were wishing me a speedy recovery and I thought that was really great. Most people, and all the other clubs, had wanted to stay right out of it, but Sy and Guitar have always been top blokes.

My mum was always there. She's the sweetest, quietest thing, but, as usual, tough. A lot of women would just fall on the floor if they lost two sons shot dead like Chop and Shadow. But she knew that she had to keep going for the three of us in hospital and she knew she had to keep our sisters in one piece, too. All my sisters live close to Mum. They can walk to her place. And she had my eldest son Chane, who was fifteen at the time, living with her too.

Lard's Mum was another good one, always making sure we were all right. Lard's brother Aspro came a lot too. The cops thought he was in the club at first, but we explained that he was just Lard's brother and had nothing to do with the club so they stopped hassling him after that.

I WAS really worried about Wack and the way his arm was healing, but the nurses were doing the best they could. I was still pretty crook myself. I still had the fever caused by four abscesses that had formed where the slugs had gone through my right lung and out my back. Someone was always putting cold cloths on my forehead.

I still managed to have a bit of a laugh despite the pain and fever. One day Lard put himself into a wheel-chair and went down to the public phones at the other end of the ward. The coppers came in and discovered he was missing. They checked the showers then freaked out. They were running all over the hospital looking for him. Meanwhile, Lard wheeled himself back to the room, put himself to bed and asked, 'What's going on with all the coppers running round everywhere?'

'They're looking for you.'

Porky cracked up. Anyway, a while later three or four cops poked their heads in the room and went off their brains. 'Where have you been, Melville?'

Lard laughed. 'I went down the fuckin' phone. Where d'ya think I've been? Out jogging? I've got half me foot blown off.'

'You could have told us where you were going.'

'Go and get fucked.'

I'D JUST had a pain-killing injection when two detectives came into the ward. They marched up to my bed. 'We're here to question you about what happened at the Viking Tavern, Campbell.' I told them to go away. I was finding it hard to keep my eyes open; the injections really knocked me about. But they kept on ranting and raving.

Lard butted in: 'Can't you cunts see me brother's in a real bad way? Get out or I'll call the matron.'

So the two Ds left. I mumbled a 'Thanks, Lard,' and went off to Disneyland.

ONE DAY I was watching Wack, who was deep in thought. 'What's up, Wack?' I asked.

'Oh, I was just thinking about Chop and Shadow, and how we were real targets that day.'

'Yeah, I know what ya mean.'

He just lay there so I said, 'Come on, Wack, Shadow and Chop wouldn't want ya worrying about 'em. They're up there having a good time. They're with the old man.'

'It's not so much that I'm worrying about 'em,' he said. 'I'm just really pissed off. You're laying over there full of fuckin' holes. I got half me arm blown up. Snake got shot in the guts. Shadow and Chop are gone. Bull was the only lucky one, and he would feel real bad about that. Six of us went out there and the rest of the club . . .'

'Nah, not all the club,' I reminded him. 'Bongo and Mouth weren't there.'

'Well all the club but them two. And they probably would've stayed up on the street anyway. When you look at it, it was the Campbells that got all the damage.'

'Yeah, but Lard got shot in the foot, and Porky's got a big hole in his leg,' I said.

'And Roach's got a broken arm,' he added. 'Who else got hurt?'

'Davo. He got stabbed.'

'I forgot about that. But even counting that, you look at it, there's still more of us copped it, because we're always up the front. I'm sick of seeing me brothers get hurt. From now on why don't we let the rest of the club do some fighting, Ceese?'

'That's just the way it is, Wack. That's the way we were brought up. It's just a pity that the tavern had to happen for us to find out who was who.'

'You're not wrong. Some of those blokes would've won a medal in the hundred-metre sprint they were that fast getting out of there.'

'Let's talk about something else,' I said.

THE NEXT day a couple of coppers came into the room. 'All of your mates have been busted for what happened out at Milperra.'

'Whaddya mean?' Wack asked.

'They've all been charged,' the senior copper said.

'With what?' Wack wanted to know.

'Ah, I can't tell you that.'

Later that night Donna came up and filled us in on what had gone down. 'They raided all the houses and busted all the blokes in the club,' she said. 'They even raided our place.'

'What'd they raid our place for?'

'They said they were looking for you.'

'Looking for me? What a load of bull.'

She said she opened the door and the coppers started pulling down all the barbed wire I'd put across the gate to the front verandah. She couldn't believe it when they claimed they were searching for me. She looked at the bloke who was doing all the talking, and said, 'He's in Bankstown Hospital. You've got two or three blokes watching him all day. Make a phone call.' But the cops just wanted an excuse to go through the place. They went in and stole whatever they wanted. She told us how they took her leather jeans, my jacket and vest, all the photo albums, all my karate and wrestling trophies. 'Three-quarters of our stuff is missing,' she said.

After Lard's mum and my sisters had left for the night, she said to me, 'You know all that money we had?'

'Yeah?'

'That's gone too.'

'Fuckin' great.'

'Yeah, every penny we had to buy the property at Bowral.'

She said a lot of the old ladies had got together to try and figure out what to do. Shadow's old lady Joanne was there too. 'And there's Joanne dolling herself up,' Donna told me. 'And I said to her, "Whaddya think you're doing?" And she goes, "Going out. I've got to take my mind off all this." And I said to her, "What about the rest of us? You don't see us running about." She just walked out and hopped into a car. You know who she went with?'

'Yeah,' I said.

'And then they were gone.'

'I'd hate to think what Shadow's thinking up there . . . Did they find the jar of fingers?' I asked. It was going to be tricky explaining the digits and the odd eyeball I had in the doghouse along with some of my tools.

'No,' she said.

'Get rid of it.'

So she got one of the blokes who was still out to help her. They dumped it all in the river.

LARD HAD been watching the coppers. He'd noticed that every morning, about eight o'clock, all nine of them went to the little room at the end of the corridor for breakfast and usually stayed there for forty-five minutes. He'd timed them over a couple of weeks.

He'd also noticed a copper out on the verandah having a smoke one day. We didn't have a door onto the verandah, but Lard opened up the huge floor-to-ceiling windows which were as good as a door, and hobbled out on his crutches to talk to this constable.

'Where's that door at the end of the balcony go?' he asked.

'I dunno,' the copper said. 'Hang on, I'll have a

look.' So the copper walked down to the end of the balcony, went through the door and came back. 'There's a set of stairs that takes you down into the garden.'

'Oh really,' said Lard, all casual.

Lard came back inside. 'Well if we ever want to escape we just found the way.'

Escape had been a long way from our minds at that point, but pretty soon after this, we heard that the coppers were going to start holding bedside courts. Bandidos had already been charged with affray and offensive behaviour after the ambush. Then there'd been the raids when more got arrested and they started charging them all with murder. They'd already held bedside courts for Jock and a few other Comancheros who were in a different hospital. And there were more arrests a few days after that. So by early October, forty blokes from both clubs had been arrested, charged with murder and locked up. Except for a couple of blokes like Bernie, who was hiding out, the only blokes who hadn't been charged were us four in Bankstown Hospital. For the life of us, we couldn't figure out what we could be arrested for, given that we'd been ambushed and were only acting in self-defence. But the cops seemed to be doing it anyhow.

I thought, Well I'm not going to jail. I haven't done anything wrong. All I did was ride into a car park, try to get some cocksucking wimps to put their guns down and then got shot. Now these coppers wanted to charge me for it. And no fuckin' way was I going to jail in the condition I was in. I could hardly move.

So I said to Lard, 'You know that way you found of getting out of here?'

'Yeah?'

'Well I think I'm gunna take it. Any of youse wanna come?'

'Nuh, I wouldn't make it,' Porky said.

Lard and Wack both said no too. I think they were pretty confident they'd beat any charges that were brought against them.

'If you want me to stay,' I said, 'I will. But if it's all right with you fellas, I'm gunna leave.'

'Go for it,' Lard said.

I told Donna that when she came back to visit me that night she should bring up some trackies, thongs and a top. 'Tomorrow, I'm gunna pull all the drips out and I'm gunna go out that window.' I told her to meet me the next morning at eight at the end of the verandah. She stuck her head out the window and saw the door. I said, 'When you're leaving, go down to the grounds out there, walk up the stairs, push the door open and make sure you can see the window here.'

'All right,' she said.

So at eight o'clock next morning, when the cops had gone for breakfast, I pulled the drips out of my arms and the tubes out of the side of my chest. I struggled into the trackies and the top.

'D'ya think you'll make it?' Lard asked.

'I've got to make it,' I said, wishing them all the best. 'Don't worry, as soon as I can look after myself I'll be seeing youse.' I lifted up the window, hopped out of it, and there at the end of the verandah I could see the door. It was only about twenty metres away but it seemed like five miles. It was the first time I'd walked since the Viking Tavern and my legs were jelly. I finally got to the door, opened it and there she was. The woman – wearing a beanie and a jacket. She helped me down the stairs and across the garden. I tried to walk as upright as possible as we went past a gardener. My mate Pancho was waiting in his Falcon. I got in the back and lay down on pillows they'd brought for me. They covered me with a blanket and drove me to Pancho's place up the back of Mount Druitt in Sydney's outer west.

Just hours after I got away, Lard, Porky and Wack were each charged with seven counts of murder.

CHAPTER 17

The day I got away from the hospital, the coppers were at pains to tell the press that I hadn't actually escaped. 'We want to stress that Colin Campbell was not under police guard himself,' they said. 'He had not been charged with anything and was perfectly entitled to sign himself out of hospital as he did. The police guard at Bankstown Hospital is for the safety and security of patients and staff.' Could have fooled me.

They tried to scare Donna by telling the papers that if I didn't get medical help I'd probably die; that I could only get the strength of antibiotic I needed in hospital. There was probably a bit of truth in it, but I wasn't going back. I was not going to go to jail for being the victim of an ambush that had killed my brothers.

Pancho and his missus, Cheryl, had set up a room for me with a double mattress and air conditioning that could point straight at me. I was still running the huge fever. Donna and Cheryl went from doctor to doctor all over Sydney complaining of infections, sore throats, coughing and spluttering, dizzy spells and pleurisy to get antibiotics for me.

They should have won Oscars for their performances. They just kept getting those pills, whatever type they could get hold of, and shovelled them into me. I was doing about twenty-five pills a day.

I might have been on the run, but we weren't really hiding too hard. My eldest sons Chane and Lee would visit me a couple of times a week. My brother Wheels kept in touch over the phone. That's how I found out that a Bandit from the States had come out to try and see either Snoddy or myself. But Mouth – who was one of the few Bandits who was free because of his mystery illness on the day of the ambush – had met the American and told him there was no way he could talk to us because it was too dangerous to meet me or go into Parklea jail where Snoddy and the others had been locked up. So we never got to see this Bandido. Mouth kept the guy away from everyone.

Snoddy smuggled a letter out of Parklea to me, telling me that Mouth wanted to make all the blokes from Griffith members – patching them straight away with no prospect time. I didn't like the idea. I only knew the names of about four of those blokes and I'd only met them once when they'd come to a party at the clubhouse in Balmain. But with Mouth putting the pressure on Snoddy, and me not being able to see him, Snoddy agreed to patch them. The concession I got from Snoddy was that if I wanted to start a chapter some time down the track, I could.

* * *

TWENTY-FIVE DAYS after I escaped, we heard that Bernie had been arrested. I had no reason to think he wouldn't be staunch like all the other blokes had been. The closest the cops had got to getting a statement out of any of us was when Big Tony got arrested. He'd been on the run a few months when he'd put an ad in the paper trying to sell his car. Somehow the coppers knew it was him and these two blokes turned up to buy the car and wanted to go for a test drive. So Tony took them for a spin and all of a sudden cop cars turned up from everywhere blocking their path and one of these blokes pulled a gun and put it to Tony's head: 'You're under arrest.' Tony turned around and said, 'I s'pose this means you don't wanna buy the car.'

They had Kid Rotten in the cop shop for hour after hour, threatening him with everything if he didn't make a statement. He refused. They did that to everyone to some extent: 'You're gunna go to jail for life. You're gunna lose your family.' But no one had given a statement or signed anything. Unlike the Comos.

So it came as a bit of a surprise when the committal hearing started – two weeks after Bernie's capture – and on the second day they rolled out Bernie as the star witness. He'd done a deal with the prosecution. He spent days on the stand telling them everything he knew. He confirmed to the court that we weren't armed, and that we were all going back to Daniel's birthday party afterwards, but he threw in some wobblies as well.

I was getting messages from my brother Wheels – who wasn't a Bandido at that time but would later join – who was going to the hearing each day at Penrith court. Wheels rang me one night and said that Bernie had been asked what he thought of me.

Wheels explained, 'He started off making you sound like you weren't a bad bloke. Like, he said you always kept the peace within the club, and he said you kept the peace between our club and other clubs.' According to Wheels, Bernie said I never went looking for fights, but that if there was a fight on I always finished them. And that I made it my job to make sure no member in the club got hurt. Which all sounded good, but then Bernie turned round out of the blue and told the magistrate, 'Oh, but Caesar's got a secret graveyard down in the Snowy Mountains.'

Wheels said the magistrate, Greg Glass, looked at Bernie a bit surprised and Bernie blurted out, 'Caesar is a contract killer on the side.' I don't know where he got that idea from, but it went into the court records, which I wasn't too happy about.

WE'D BEEN staying at Pancho and Cheryl's place for a while and I didn't want to get them into shit if the coppers found me. So in early 1985 I asked Pancho to find me a place somewhere down near Bowral in the Southern Highlands south of Sydney. It was still close to my family, and Donna would have people around who could help her. So he found a joint at Hill Top and it turned out to be a nice little place. He got my dogs for me and brought them down. And that's what I mean when I say the cops mustn't have tried very hard to find me. As far as I was concerned, I wasn't on the run. I'd done nothing wrong. We rented this place in my name. Donna was on the pension in the name of Donna Campbell. She'd go into Mittagong to do the shopping, and come back in a taxi. All they had to do was check where she was picking up her pension, or check the real-estate agents. I could've found myself in a week.

My son Lee, who was then fourteen and a half, used to come down to visit for weeks at a time. He'd do the cloak-and-dagger thing, catching a few different buses then the train, and we'd have someone pick him up at Bowral.

We went though some hard times at Hill Top. Donna was carrying the world on her back. And being out of the city, it was much harder to find different doctors for her antibiotics performances. Here I was, flat on my back, for the first time counting on someone else to look out for me. It had always been the other way around – I looked out for everyone else. My whole right side was fucked, my right lung had four big holes in it. I could not lift my arm for months. All I could do was lie on the bed. But with Donna's help I started to get the arm working. She put a small tin of baked beans in a plastic bag which I used to do arm curls. Over time, I worked my way up to a big Coke bottle. All the time I knew she was worrying that I was trying too hard. She also knew what I had on my mind.

I don't ever forget and I always get even no matter how long it takes. She knew me better than anyone and she knew the things I'd do to even up, but she was worried that my back was becoming infected. I had four big, painful lumps back there. They were getting that bad I had to lie on my stomach or my side. It felt like the slugs were just under the skin and if you nicked them with a razor blade they might just pop out.

So Donna, being an ex-nurse, decided that they had to go. And being my wife and best friend I knew there was no one better to do it. She'd done it years earlier with the .22 bullet and we didn't think this would be any harder. So she went to the Hill Top shopping centre, bought some Dettol, Gem razor blades, sutures to stitch me up, antibiotic powder, and a needle. Then she went to the bottle shop for a cask of wine to steady her nerves.

The next afternoon, I sat at the kitchen table, which Donna had rubbed down with Dettol. She took my singlet off, put towels under the chair and on the floor. Luckily it was a tiled floor.

As she cut into the first lump, I gripped the table with my left arm. I could feel the skin peeling apart as the blade cut down. She took a sip of wine to calm herself. She said it was much harder doing this on someone she loved than just any patient in a hospital. She cut down further and hit a blob of gunk. She stopped and got it all out. 'That's what I've found,' she said, depositing the blob of green jelly on the table. 'Do you want me to go further?' We'd never seen anything like this stuff. It wasn't pus.

'Seeing you've opened it up you might as well keep going,' I said.

She took another swig and cut some more, then more swigs and more cuts while I gripped the table with my good arm. As she went deeper, it became hard for her to keep the skin apart with all the blood getting in the way. But she kept on slicing down until at last – about two inches under the skin, she hit metal. Only it wasn't a straightforward lump of lead. This thing had grown into a ball of gristle.

By now I could see blood running off my back onto my sides and down to the floor.

'Do you want me to keep going?' she said. 'Because I can't reach it with the razor. I'll have to use your buck knife.'

'Go for it,' I said.

Donna held the little blade over a flame, then splashed it with Dettol and in she went.

That's when the pain really kicked in and the blood flowed as she tried to pry this thing out. The four-inch blade was halfway in as she cut around the gristle until, pop, she had it out. It turned out to be an SG 00 from a twelve-gauge shotgun.

That done, Donna started on the second one – cutting it open, squeezing out the green stuff, digging out the slug with the buck knife and the razor, then stopping the bleeding and filling it up with antibiotic powder, before sewing it all together.

Two hours later, she was stitching up the fourth one, and I'd just about had it. The pain was exhausting. She helped me into bed.

'I don't know how you did it,' she said. 'I was shaking and felt like screaming, but you didn't make a sound.'

'Don't worry, I wanted to,' I said.

I lay there on my stomach and did my best to get some sleep while Donna did her best to clean up the blood from the floor and the table. It took her more than half a day.

A day later, though, I was still bleeding, so she opened me up again and stitched me back up afresh. This time the bleeding stopped and the wound healed without even a tiny bit of infection. Donna was still getting all my antibiotics from her multiple doctor visits. She was one sick woman.

CHAPTER 18

As I started to recover I began to think about forming another chapter of the Bandidos. I wanted a bunch of blokes out there that would do anything to defend the club's name. Almost all the blokes I'd been riding with were locked up. And I didn't trust Mouth. So ever since I'd heard about the Griffith chapter, I'd been thinking about getting my own going.

I would kick it off with a couple of prospects and I would be president. I could've started the chapter by myself but I wanted to do it properly. I'd never used the fact I was sergeant-at-arms – or that I'd worn the first set of colours in Australia – to get my way. I always went along with what the majority of the club voted, even if I didn't like it. So I sent my brother Wheels to Parklea to ask Snoddy if it was all right with him.

Snoddy knew I wasn't too happy about the Griffith chapter being patched up so he gave me the go ahead.

275

One of the first blokes I got in was Sheepskin. He'd been ringing me ever since he left the Comos in the weeks before the ambush. And when I was in hospital he sent cards. Donna said that he also rocked up each week to check she was all right. He'd said to her, 'Tell Ceese if there's anything I can do for him, or if there's anyone he wants taken care of, I'll do it.' So there was him, plus my former brother-in-law, Lurch, who'd been a Gladiator, my brother Wheels and my mates Pancho, who was an ex-Hells Angel, and Russell. Roach joined up from jail and later Sparksy and my brother Snake came over too.

During this time, I was talking to the president and sergeant-at-arms of an outlaw club in Victoria. The sergeant had been a big help in letting me know what was going on. Like, he told me how they were at a party with the Griffith Bandidos and Mouth was there telling everyone how he'd been to the States to see the Bandidos over there. And how when the Bandido from the States had come out to see how we were going, the only Bandido he saw was him – implying that he, Mouth, was the main man and that Snoddy and I didn't count any more. The other club thought it was a bit funny that he would be discussing club business and running down other members in front of everyone.

After checking around, I found out where Mouth was living and got a phone number. I rang him and told him, 'You go round bad-mouthing me to anyone, I'll rip your colours off your back. Not just for bad-mouthing me, but if you think I don't know what you've been doing you're a bigger arsehole than what you look.'

'What are you talking about?'

'I know you've been rooting Joanne. I know you did it not long after Shadow was buried. I also know you're rooting _____ [another member's old lady] too while her fella's locked up. You were supposed to be really tight with the bloke.'

Mouth denied it.

'You can deny it all you want,' I said. 'I've got people out there who know. So you've got two choices. I come round your place and take your colours, or you hand them in.'

Mouth just disappeared after that. As far as I'm concerned he stopped being a Bandido that day. No one has seen him round the club since.

It was 28 April 1985, almost eight months after the ambush. Donna and I were watching the news, but I wish I hadn't been. It came up that the president of the Bandidos Motorcycle Club, Anthony 'Snoddy' Spencer, had committed suicide in Parklea prison.

After about an hour of just sitting there blankly in front of the box, Donna said, 'Why do you think he did it?'

I thought there were probably a couple of reasons. He probably blamed himself for Shadow and Chop's deaths and having the club end up where it did. And he wasn't stupid, he knew what had happened to Shadow's old lady. That would have added to his torment.

I wish he hadn't done it. Snoddy gave up his life when he had it there to live. I had two brothers who died for the club. I was pissed off with Snoddy for doing what he did, but then again, I'd never been to jail so I couldn't understand what was going through his brain. I just wish he'd have waited.

I had got word to him that I was eventually going to hand myself in. I knew my duty was to be inside with my brothers so I could take care of them. But I didn't want to go to jail until my arm was strong enough for me to look after myself. I wasn't going to put myself at the mercy of halfwit standover men inside. I know if I'd been there with him he probably wouldn't have done it. But as the old saying goes, shit happens.

A FEW weeks after Snoddy's death, Donna went to the little shopping centre in Hill Top to buy some hot chips when, wouldn't you know it, she ran into someone who knew us – Bushy. He was an original Bandido who had left the club when the war got too hot. She came back and told me, all upset that he might ring the cops.

'I don't reckon he will,' I said.

'But you never know.'

I knew Bushy wouldn't have handed me in, but I knew that he would probably tell someone and they'd probably tell someone else, and word would eventually get out. While I wasn't trying too hard to avoid the law, it didn't mean I wanted to get caught. So next thing I knew, Donna was on the blower to Pancho and Cheryl, who had just moved to Perth. We decided we'd move there too – immediately. Just a day or two earlier, one of my brothers had given us an XC 351 Ford panel van to use in case of an emergency. We threw as much stuff into it as Donna could manage, plus one of our three dogs, and within the hour we were ready to go. Chane was with us and it was a tearful goodbye, leaving him behind.

Donna couldn't drive then so I had to do it all. We slept in the car – the two adults, two kids, the dog Buck and all the gear. You could never get comfortable with a fan sticking in your ribs or someone else squirming about. Donna was still bottle feeding Lacey. It was a tough trip, so monotonous, but we did it in four and a half days. We arrived at Bayswater, Perth, where Cheryl was waiting for us and we followed her back to their place. Our friends put us up for about three weeks, then we rented a place a few blocks away at Shakespeare Street, Mount Hawthorn. We signed the lease in my name. We enrolled Daniel in school. Donna got a job in the classifieds department at the *Western Mail* newspaper. She used to work at the *Telegraph* in Sydney so she knew her stuff, and after only about three weeks there they made her a supervisor and later a manager.

It was still my intention to hand myself in when I got strong enough. Pancho came around just about every day to help me train so I could get the muscle back in my right arm, which was still a withered mess.

JUST BEFORE Christmas 1985, thirteen months after the committal hearing had begun, it finished with forty Bandits and Comos committed to stand trial for murder. Only two of the forty-two who'd been charged weren't sent for trial – Snoddy and my brother Wack.

Wack had been crook ever since Milperra. After all the surgeries and everything he just never recovered.

They still put him in Parklea, but for about six or seven months he complained of chest pains and not feeling right. They only had nurses on there most of the time; a doctor came in once a fortnight or something. He was looking about eighty years old and way past his use-by date. The nurse kept telling Wack that he just had bronchitis. Finally he got so crook they sent him into Prince Henry Hospital and he was diagnosed with cardiomyopathy. His heart was swelling and getting too big for his chest. The specialist told him that if he'd come in six months earlier he would've been able to do something. He was put on the waiting list for a heart transplant and was positioned near the top of the list. But then one day he rocked up at the hospital with a Bandidos T-shirt on, and a couple of the nurses said, 'Oh, you're one of those blokes from Milperra, are you?'

'Yeah.'

The next thing we knew he'd been dropped down the waiting list.

There hadn't been much in the Perth papers about the committal hearing so I didn't know a lot about it. Even so, I was surprised that the Bandits didn't get off. I thought the Comos would go down because they'd turned up with shotguns and waited for us with walkie-talkies and the whole lot. They'd obviously come there with the intention of committing a crime. We'd gone there with the intention of buying some bike parts and watching a band. I mean, did the magistrate honestly think that we'd gone there to shoot up all these people with the plan of then turning round to ride back to my young fella's birthday party, where ten cars could pull up in the street straight alongside our backyard and empty as many shotguns as they wanted into our women and children?

Suddenly, it looked like the club was going to go to jail for a long time. Snoddy was dead. I started to feel weak that I was out while they were all inside. We needed to keep the guys strong and together. They needed a leader.

My arm was still a long way off being any good for fighting, but, being big-headed, I figured I was better with one arm than most blokes with two, so I decided I was going to hand myself in.

I talked it over with Donna then got my mum and my sister, Patricia, to get me a QC. Patricia put me on to Dr Greg Woods. I'd heard of him, so I agreed with that. I spoke to him and we made arrangements that I'd come back, meet him and hand myself in. We started trying to arrange for a place for Donna and the kids to stay in Sydney.

It was a stinking hot summer in Perth. One afternoon, a few days after we started making plans to come back, I was out on the front verandah, watching my bull terrier Buck run around and do his business.

Unbeknown to me, a bloke had broken out of the Perth lock-up that day and as it happened his parents lived in the same street as us. So three or four blokes from the Consorting Squad decided to pay his parents a visit. The only cops in Western Australia who had a photo of me just happened to be the Consorting Squad. They drove right by and nothing happened.

But around five o'clock the next morning, 18 February 1986, Donna and I were lying on a double mattress on the lounge room floor – because it was cooler in there than in the bedroom – when we heard a dirty great banging on the front door. She thought it was the Comos. I looked out the window and saw coppers everywhere, shotguns, flak jackets, navy blue jumpsuits.

The pounding on the door continued as they tried to batter it down. But the door at the front of the house had been put on backwards, so they were actually bashing the door where the hinges were. They were really struggling. *Bang bang bang*. It gave me time to get into my trackies and put on a singlet while Donna went and got the kids. I was waiting in the lounge room for them when they burst in. The first one came running at me with a shotgun like he was going to hit me in the head with it. I still couldn't use my right arm but let him have one with the left and dropped him.

Maybe I should have gone peacefully, but that's just me. If someone comes running at me, I just go off. If they'd knocked on the door and said, 'Are you Colin Caesar Campbell?' I would have just said, 'Yeah.' But not now.

Bang. I dropped another one, then kicked another in the ribs. I put down about six or seven of them before one copper yelled out, 'If you don't stop there could be an accident.' I looked over and here was this copper with a shotgun pointed at my young bloke Daniel's head. 'If you don't calm down this gun could go off.' And then another copper stepped up and pointed one at Donna.

'Yeah, all right,' I said. 'Youse have got me.'

The lounge room was filling up with coppers and then four Ds came in.

'You're Colin Caesar Campbell?' the head detective said.

'Yeah.'

'Can you step over here?'

I remained on guard but stepped over to the corner of the lounge room with him, and he spoke calmly.

'If you quieten down and cooperate with us, I'll guarantee you that nothing will happen to your wife or kids. They won't be charged.

'I'm not making any statements.'

'Well, we'll talk about that later.' So two coppers came over and tried handcuffing me but my right arm wouldn't go round my back. I kept telling them I couldn't move it. The detective said, 'Don't put his hands behind his back. Handcuff them in front.'

He was being extra nice.

'Will you let my wife make one phone call?' I asked.

'No.'

Some of the coppers went to go out the back door. I tried to stop them. 'Don't go out there. The dog'll eat ya.'

They went out anyway and Buck was straight into them. He latched onto one copper's leg and once a bull terrier latches on, that's it. The way Donna told it to me was that Buck knocked this copper over and swung himself around so that the bulk of the dog's body was on top of the copper. The other five officers out there couldn't shoot him because they'd most likely hit their mate. So they just laid into him with the butts of their shotguns. Donna eventually got him off and let him out the back gate so there wouldn't be any more trouble. I used to take him for a walk every afternoon up to Pancho's place so he ran straight there. Pancho saw the blood dripping off him and knew something was wrong, so he flew down to our place.

By the time he got there I'd been taken away.

THE DS took me into the cop shop and were nice as pie. They offered me sandwiches and a soft drink and were all chatty. They wanted to know what had happened on the day of the ambush. I told them I wasn't saying or signing anything. They had me there for about eight or nine hours when a D walked in and said, 'Your mate's downstairs. He says he's not leaving till he sees ya.'

So they let Pancho up to see me and Donna was with him. She gave me a big hug and Pancho asked how I was going.

'As good as can be expected.'

'Are they belting ya?'

'Not so far.'

The cops let Donna give me my medication then ushered her and Pancho out.

'Well, if you're not going to sign anything,' they said, 'you're going down to the cells.'

Four uniformed coppers came and took me down into the bowels of the building. They walked me into a cell and handcuffed me to the bars at the front. Two of them grabbed hold of one leg each while the other two came up close to my body. *Whump*. The first guy hit me once. Then *whump*, the second one had a go. They started taking turns, whacking me in the back, in the side of the head, up under the arm. My right arm was killing me but they were only young blokes and I wasn't going to give in to them.

'My grandmother can hit harder than you,' I said. That didn't go down too well and I thought to myself, Why don't you keep your big mouth shut?

Then the two that were holding my legs said they wanted their go at the big bad bikie. So they swapped over and the fresh pair started using me as their punching bag.

I kept egging them on so they kept laying in. I didn't know how much more I could take, but then an older woman walked into the cell. She must have been approaching sixty, looked like a secretary, but at the sight of her these young coppers sprang to attention.

'What do you think you're up to?' she snapped, looking me over and seeing blood on my head. 'The four of you out of this cell. If I see any of you with this man again you'll all be up at Geraldton by the next morning.' I didn't have a clue where Geraldton was but she made it sound like a pretty bad place to be.

She grabbed two sergeants – one male, one female – and said, 'I'm going to leave this gentleman in your care. If he gets even one more scratch on him, you two will be going to Geraldton.'

Everything was sweet after that. The female sergeant would bring me Hungry Jack's burgers and thick shakes, the whole bit. The Ds kept being nice to me. They'd bring me up from the cells each day for about an hour and a half and put me in a room upstairs. They let Donna and the kids in. This head detective kept saying to me, 'See how good coppers are? We're not as bad as people think.'

'Oh yeah, what about the beating I copped down in the cells?' I said to him.

'Oh, I heard about that. They were only young fellas, new to the force.'

There was another D playing bad cop and he said to me one time, 'You better cooperate or else you know what we can do to you.'

'Youse have already done it,' I said.

I spent about five days in the cells waiting for two Ds from New South Wales to rock up. Then I was put before the court and charged with one count of murder – that of my own brother, Shadow. I was gutted. You couldn't hurt me any more. Apparently the coppers had decided that the way they were going to lock all of us up for a very long time was to make a case that we had a common purpose: that we were basically all co-conspirators to the events in the car park that day and that, therefore, we were all responsible for all seven deaths. So they were charging everyone who was there with all seven murders, but for the extradition they kept it simple and only used one. They could have chosen any of the deaths to hit me with but they were obviously trying to get some sort of a reaction out of me by charging me with killing Shadow.

The hearing was just a formality and I didn't fight it. But then none of the airlines wanted to take me. There were stories in the Perth papers about how the airlines were afraid of retaliation from my brothers. I asked one of the coppers what the problem was.

'They've all read the papers about how Caesar Campbell was the standover man for the Bandidos,' he said. 'And how you had a secret graveyard in the Snowy Mountains where you've been burying bodies for over twenty years.'

'What a load of shit,' I said. 'It's only been fifteen years.'

IT LOOKED like I was going to be returning by train, but then at the last minute one of the airlines agreed to fly me. It was quite a relief because I didn't want to have to spend three days handcuffed to a copper.

I was allowed to change into my own clothes. So I was dressed in the usual black jeans, black boots, shirt, bandana and sunnies. I was put in an unmarked van full of cops and taken to the airport. The head of airport security wanted to meet me, so I had to go through that. Then they walked me out through a big hangar. We stopped about every thirty feet until someone said, 'Clear', then we'd go the next thirty feet. This went all the way from the hangar to the back of the plane where there were about twenty coppers standing with guns. I was led up the stairway at the back of the plane, then plonked into the middle of the very back row of seats. I had one detective handcuffed to my right hand and one to my left. This was going to be a great flight.

They let the other passengers on and we hadn't been in the air long when one of the Ds turned to me and said they had an offer to make me. 'If you help us out, we can give you a grand a week and relocation to anywhere in the world – with a new identity.'

'No way, shove it up your arses,' I said.

'How about a hundred thousand dollars up front, a thousand a week and the relocation?'

'I'm not talking to you.'

'You know Bernie's already rolled over on you.'

'Yeah, I know what the cunt's done.'

'Well he's only getting fifty thousand, and five hundred a week. We're offering you double.'

'You can offer me a million dollars, I'm not turning on anyone in me club. I started the club. I can't wait to be back with me brothers. What you coppers and straights don't understand about outlaw clubs is that we live for the brotherhood. We live for the loyalty and honour of being there for each other no matter what. There is not a thing you can offer me, nothing you can do to me. I was the first to wear Bandido colours in Australia and you will never know what that means or feels like.'

They ordered something to eat but didn't get me anything, mongrels. I was starving.

With the handcuffs on, my hands had to move with their hands as they ate. So every time they lifted up the hand that I was cuffed to, I happened to have to sneeze or scratch my ear; I'd jerk my hand and food would go everywhere so that both of them ended up with spills over their shirts and on their trousers. They gave the meals back half-eaten.

They kept on at me about the deal. Said I could go anywhere in Australia or to England, Canada, New Zealand. A thousand dollars a week was a lot of money back then. They said they might even be able to get me a fair sum more up front and in the bank.

'There's no way I'm gunna do what that cocksucker Bernie did. I'm not giving up me brothers.'

If I'd been asked who I thought would have ratted on the club, I wouldn't have picked Bernie. I thought he'd stay staunch. But, like I've said to other blokes, I can kind of understand where he was coming from.

The cops had Bernie for ten days and they moved him from cop shop to cop shop so no solicitor could get near him. And his missus, Caroline, hated the club. She was a real north shore tennis type and they'd just had a son. Apparently she threatened Bernie that it was either the club or her and the son. I know I'd tell them to punch it. But after ten days of being pounded and having your missus coming in and telling you it's your son or the club, I can see the pressure he was under. At least I know Donna would never put me in that situation. Even so, I could never have ratted on the club. Every morning you've got to get up and look at yourself in the mirror.

As WE approached Sydney Airport, the jacks said, 'When we land, just sit here and don't move. We're going to be last off the plane. Be as inconspicuous as you can.'

The plane landed, the door at the front opened. I don't think a single person had got off before a great herd of Tactical Response Group coppers came running down the aisle with shotguns.

I turned to the two Ds. 'This is being inconspicuous, is it?'

We went out through the back of the plane. There were probably twenty-five coppers on the tarmac, vans everywhere, carloads of Ds. I was bundled into a van and taken to Waverley Court and put in a cell, still in handcuffs. A copper from the Homicide Squad came up to me and said, 'I'm going to offer you the deal one more time – a new house, a thousand dollars a week.'

I told him to stick it up his arse so he gave me a few thumps. I told him he hit like a girl. I always had to have the last word. He took a few more swings until one of the coppers outside yelled, 'They want him up in court.'

I was taken up to the courtroom. It was just a formality and the magistrate remanded me to Parklea prison. Then back downstairs and into the van. I could see the TRG blokes getting into a van in front and others getting into a van behind. A trail of police cars joined in.

My mind was running through what it might be like in jail. I'd never been in one before. I'd only had that one charge from when Irene's boyfriend fell off the roof.

I wondered what the guards would be like. I'd heard all the stories. But I figured they'd probably be like cops: there'd be some bad ones and some good ones. Well, what can they do? I thought to myself. Give me a thumping? You've had plenty of people try that before. I figured I'd let them know that if they tried to thump me they were going to cop it back in spades. I'd also tell them: 'You be fair with me and I'll be fair with you.'

We eventually pulled up and I could hear someone saying, 'You're going to have to hand your guns in, boys. We can't let you through the gate with those.' We were at Parklea. There was a long wait as all these coppers handed in their guns. Finally a gate opened and the truck drove through, turned around and backed up, beeping, into a dock.

The van door opened and I stood up, all in black with the sunglasses and the bandana. Lined up in front of me, to the left and right, was a big line of Tactical Response Group coppers in black pyjamas, helmets and bullet-proof vests. Black batons raised. It was like they were waiting for the Incredible Hulk.

Life had just taken a whopping great turn.

But that's a whole other story, which I may or may not tell . . . one day.

CHAPTER 19

FEBRUARY, 1986

Walking into the main compound of Parklea jail gave me one of the best sights I'd seen in eighteen months. Bandidos everywhere, coming to greet me. I was back with my brothers, blood and Bandido, reunited while we awaited trial.

Before we even got to court, eight of our blokes were no-billed, which meant the murder charges against them were dropped and they walked out of jail, facing only the minor charge of affray. We couldn't work out why the eight were picked. It was like they'd just chosen the names from a hat. One of them was my brother Snake and he'd done pretty much what I did – walked down and told the Comos to fight like men, then got shot. My name was never going to be picked out though. My barrister told me the coppers were gunning for me and Jock.

The trial was an extravaganza. All the Bandidos in one perspex-screened box, all the Comos in another, thirty-two different barristers and solicitors. There were sixty-four coppers on security. They reckoned it cost the state ten million big ones.

The whole thing lasted over a year: April 1986 to June 1987. But I knew after six weeks that we were going to be found guilty. So I just sat up in the last seat in the back row and leant into the corner, arms folded, feet up on the seat in front of me, sunglasses on. The Rodent (Justice Adrian Roden) hated it; he couldn't tell whether I was sleeping or watching. Sometimes he'd get the court officers to check on me. I was awake the whole time.

One day in court, homicide detective Aarne Tees came up to me and said, 'If the Comos had've done what you lot did and refused to sign a statement, we would never have been able to arrest any of you.' In trying to get us locked up, the Comancheros got themselves locked up too.

People tried to say Jock was a target that day at Milperra. Well, it came out in court that the Comos were sitting at the Viking Tavern with their shotguns and walkie-talkies for an hour before we turned up. So to say that Jock was a target was just rubbish. We didn't even know there were going to be Comos there. If I'd have known, we wouldn't have gone.

Six Campbells went to the Viking Tavern that day, and five got shot. There's your target. (And to this day I think Bull carries a big load on his shoulders that he was the only one that didn't even cop a nick.)

All of us on trial were charged with one count of affray and seven counts of murder, for the deaths of Chop and Shadow, Comancheros Foghorn, Sparra, Leroy and Dog, plus Leanne Walters. Eight Comos, including Jock, were convicted of those charges, along with just one Bandido, Lard. (The murder convictions were later downgraded to manslaughter on appeal.) The rest of us were found guilty of affray and seven counts of manslaughter – all except Knuckles, who was still recovering from his bike accident and was acquitted of the murder and manslaughter charges and found guilty only of affray. He walked free from court the day of the verdict, although like the true Bandido he was, he didn't want to leave his brothers. The rest of us went back to jail, me sentenced to seven years' non-parole.

FOUR MONTHS after the verdicts, one of the screws came up to me in jail and said, 'I'd like to see you out the front of the visiting area.'

I walked out the front and as soon as I saw my mum there I had a bad feeling. Then they told me my young brother, Wack, had died. I lost it. I wrecked half the vending machines in the visiting complex. The screw in charge of security could have had his squad jump on me, but he let me go. Never charged me with anything.

After my dad died I'd sort of stepped into his shoes, and because Wack was one of the youngest I felt real bad that I hadn't protected him better. That was the third time in my life I shed a tear.

I'd already lost two brothers fighting for the club in the car park of the Viking Tavern, and now it was three. Wack didn't die directly from his injuries, but if he hadn't been shot, his body would have had more strength to fight, and if he hadn't been in jail he would have received the right treatment earlier. So I consider that Wack laid down his life for the club, too. And there is no greater honour than dying for your club in a war. In fact, when any new member joins the Bandidos I believe they should be told the story of how Chop, Shadow and Wack died. That way they will truly know what honour, courage and brotherhood mean to the club.

POSTSCRIPT

The whole four years I was locked up, Donna didn't leave the house other than to do the shopping or visit me. When I got paroled on 6 March 1990, the first thing I did was get Donna pregnant and the second thing I did was give her the proper white wedding I knew she'd always wanted.

I saw her coming out in the dress, and I'm not ashamed to say I went all weak at the knees. We've been together thirty-one years now, and we're aiming for thirty-one more. As each year goes by I only love her more. Donna was with me when I was a Gladiator, she came through the Comancheros with me, and she was the original Bandido old lady. She's been through all the hardships, the club wars, me being shot and going to jail, and through all of that our relationship has only got stronger.

Our youngest daughter Chyanne was born in November 1990, and if I were a straight, maybe that's where the story would end. Peacefully. But I'm not a straight. I've copped more bullets since leaving jail than I did at Milperra. Donna's pulled out everything from SG 00s, the biggest shotgun pellets, down to .22s and .223s. There was a .38 once and a .45. I've still got some in my body. One worked its own way out into my ear canal while Donna was writing this book. Anytime I have to go for an X-ray the technician usually says to me, 'Oh, do you know you've been shot?'

One time they tested me for lead poisoning because of all the slugs inside me.

That's why I agreed to move out of the city. The idea was that if I was in the country people would forget about me. But then I was standing in our rural front yard watering the garden and a car pulled up. *Bang, bang.* Shot twice in the stomach. Then there were a couple more episodes of bullets coming through the house and I thought, Oh fuck it, might as well be in Sydney with my brothers.

My old man always said that no matter how good you are there's always someone better out there; it was just a question of how long it took you to run into them. When I was in my forties it started to worry me that I'd meet that bloke, but I was more worried that I'd hurt somebody and end up back inside. In my fifties I started to mellow. I'm in my sixties now, missing a quarter of a lung, and I still haven't run into him. I've never even been knocked off my feet. Not even in the car park at Milperra. Age will get me though. I'm still getting into blues with blokes in their twenties wanting to take on the big bad bikie. I'm sick and tired of it.

And the cops have never let me forget Milperra. In

December 2009, while Donna was writing this book, I had eight of them wearing all the bullet-proof gear try to bash down the door. I went and opened it before they did too much damage and they stuck their guns in my face. Spent three hours searching the place for handguns, saying I was planning my revenge on the Comos. But I swore to Mum and Donna when I got out of jail that I wouldn't touch the Comos unless they came after me. And if you've gathered nothing else from this book, you'd at least know that I'm a man of my word.

I'm proud to say that my two sons, Caspar (Lee) and Doc (Daniel), are continuing the Campbell tradition of being able to look after themselves. Caspar was the first son of a Bandido to also become a Bandido.

Together with Chane and my brothers' kids, they will proudly carry on the family name.

ACKNOWLEDGEMENTS

I would like to thank Mark and Amy for all their help and patience with writing the book, and Tom Gilliatt for taking me on board. I really appreciate your help.

And thanks to Caesar's brothers Big Bear, Witch and Crash.